Kids' TRAVEL GUIDE
to the 23rd Psalm

Group

Loveland, Colorado

group.com

Group resources actually work!

This Group resource incorporates our R.E.A.L. approach to ministry. It reinforces a growing friendship with Jesus, encourages long-term learning, and results in life transformation, because it's

Relational
Learner-to-learner interaction enhances learning and builds Christian friendships.

Experiential
What learners experience through discussion and action sticks with them up to 9 times longer than what they simply hear or read.

Applicable
The aim of Christian education is to equip learners to be both hearers and doers of God's Word.

Learner-based
Learners understand and retain more when the learning process takes into consideration how they learn best.

Kids' Travel Guide to the 23rd Psalm
Copyright © 2009 Group Publishing, Inc.

Visit our website: group.com

Credits
Contributing Authors: Gwyn D. Borcherding, Teryl Cartwright, Jan Kershner, and Roxanne Wieman
Cover and Illustrations: Rob McClurkan

Unless otherwise indicated, all Scripture quotations are taken from the *Holy Bible* New Living Translation, copyright © 1996, 2004, 2007. Used by permission of Tyndale House Publishers, Inc. Carol Stream, Illinois 60188. All rights reserved.

Library of Congress Cataloging-in-Publication Data
Kids' travel guide to the 23rd Psalm.
    p. cm.
  ISBN 978-0-7644-4005-2 (pbk. : alk. paper)
  1. Bible. O.T. Psalms XXIII--Juvenile literature. I. Group Publishing. II. Title
BS145023rd 2009
223'.20071--dc22

                            2009037561

10 9 8 7 6 5 4   18 17 16 15 14 13 12 11

Printed in the United States of America

Table of Contents

An Introduction to the Travel Guide

The graciousness and peace of the 23rd Psalm make it one of the most loved passages of the Bible. But the comfort it promises isn't just for times of peace when life is good and we're certain of God's presence. Instead it reassures us most vividly of God's protection and loving care in our most difficult times—in the darkest valley and in the presence of our enemies. *Kids' Travel Guide to the 23rd Psalm* seeks to reassure children that they can trust God's love for them in every circumstance.

Children will learn that, like the good shepherd, Jesus guides us into the abundant life God wants to give us. Like the good shepherd, he also provides for us. But his provision is more than food and water—it is "living water' and eternal life.

Kids' Travel Guide to the 23rd Psalm is designed to be applicable to kids in grades kindergarten through fifth grade. Following an overview of the 23rd Psalm, the lessons explore each phrase of the psalm in depth and lead children from God's provision in peaceful valleys and his nearness in darkest valleys—to the abundant blessings we receive as we follow him all the days of our lives.

During this 13-week journey, each child will complete a **Travel Journal.** The Travel Journal will serve as a keepsake so kids can continue to remember the concepts of the 23rd Psalm, especially of God's all-encompassing love for each one of them.

The **Pathway Point** is the central concept that children will explore and apply to their lives. The **In-Focus Verse** refers to a specific phrase of the 23rd Psalm. A **Travel Itinerary** introduces the lesson and explains how the lesson will impact children's lives.

Please read each lesson thoroughly, and make a model for the crafts before class. If you do, your lessons will flow much more smoothly. The time recommendations are only guidelines. They'll change according to how many are in your group, how prepared you are, and how much help you have. Choose activities or adapt them based on the size of your group and the time you have during your class.

Each lesson starts with a **Departure Prayer.** These are creative prayer activities that help introduce the topic and focus children on God. **Tour Guide Tips** are helps for the teacher, and **Scenic Routes** provide additional creative options.

First Stop Discoveries introduce the children to the lesson's topic. The **Story Excursions** are Bible events or Scripture passages that illustrate a Bible truth to support each concept. Kids will experience the Bible in creative and varied

ways. Choose what you think will best meet your children's needs. The activities in **Adventures in Growing** lead the children into further application of the Pathway Point. Each week, ask the children if they had opportunities to demonstrate the previous week's Pathway Point in their lives. This will be an important faith-growing time.

Souvenirs are photocopiable paper activities. Have children collect these and keep them in a notebook or folder. When your study on the 23rd Psalm is complete, each child will have a Travel Journal keepsake to use as a reminder of all he or she has learned. Each lesson closes with a **Home Again Prayer**, which offers a time of commitment and a time to ask God to direct kids' lives.

Any time during your lesson, read the **Fun Facts** section to the kids. These provide examples of the lesson's point with familiar and not-so-familiar facts.

May this exploration of the 23rd Psalm bring you and the children to a deeper realization of God's great love for you. May God surprise you with blessings in unexpected places.

The Lord Is My Shepherd

Pathway Point: God loves and watches over us.

In-Focus Verse: "The Lord is my shepherd; I have all that I need. He lets me rest in green meadows; he leads me beside peaceful streams. He renews my strength. He guides me along right paths, bringing honor to his name. Even when I walk through the darkest valley, I will not be afraid, for you are close beside me. Your rod and your staff protect and comfort me. You prepare a feast for me in the presence of my enemies. You honor me by anointing my head with oil. My cup overflows with blessings. Surely your goodness and unfailing love will pursue me all the days of my life, and I will live in the house of the Lord forever" (Psalm 23).

Travel Itinerary

Psalm 23 is one of the most well-known and often-quoted psalms in the Bible. Its message of comfort and reassurance is welcome at any time in life.

Use this lesson to help kids realize that the 23rd Psalm speaks directly to them. Show them that God knows what they face in their lives, and that he's right there with them—whether they're tired, facing decisions, or even afraid.

Help your kids see that God, our loving shepherd, wants us to be with him forever.

TOUR GUIDE TIP The experiences in this book have been designed for multi-age groups. Select from the experiences, or adapt them as needed for your kids.

DEPARTURE PRAYER (up to 5 minutes)

Set out a supply of scrap paper, and have kids form a circle.

Say: **Think about some problems you're facing right now; then take a few pieces of paper, and on each one write a word that describes a different problem. When you're done, scrunch each paper into a ball. You'll need these in a minute.**

Items to Pack: scrap paper, pens or pencils, a beach towel

Choose two kids to hold the ends of the beach towel up in the air so it's flat. Say: **Our towel-holders will hold the towel in the air like a bridge for us to go under. As each person goes under the towel, he or she will pause a moment or two, and the rest of us will toss our paper "problems" in the air over the towel. When you toss, just call out a problem, then pick up another paper problem and do the same thing. Keep doing this until everyone has gone under the towel. Remember, we're tossing up into the air, not throwing at anyone. Okay? Here we go.**

If this game gets a little loud—have fun with it! Kids will have fun, and they'll remember what they've learned.

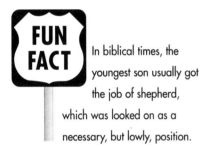

In biblical times, the youngest son usually got the job of shepherd, which was looked on as a necessary, but lowly, position.

Items to Pack: Bible, white paper, white or light-colored crayons, dark crayons, paper clips

Form a line on one side of the towel, and let kids take turns ducking under the towel, pausing, and moving to the other side. As each child goes under the towel, other kids will toss their paper wads into the air, pick up new paper wads from the floor, and continue to throw them into the air and call out problems. During the game, rotate kids to hold the towel so everyone gets a chance to walk under it.

After a few minutes, call time. Ask kids to gather the paper problems and sit in a circle with you. Make sure everyone has at least one.

Ask: • **What was it like to be under the towel when the paper problems were flying?**

• **How is this like the way God loves and cares for us?**

Say: **Just as the towel gave us protection in our game, God's love for us is kind of like an umbrella that gives us protection in real life. Of course, some of you got bonked on the head in our game. And in life, we all face problems sometimes. But even if God allows problems, he's always, always with us.** **God loves and watches over us.**

Let's thank God for his wonderful and powerful love. We'll go around the circle, and each person will place a paper problem in the middle of the circle and thank God for loving us when we face that particular problem. You may want to say something like, "Thank you, God, for loving us when we face problems at school." No matter how many paper wads you have, just say one problem. I'll start.

Begin the prayer by placing a paper wad in the circle and thanking God for being with us when we face the problem you name. Then go around the circle and let each child contribute. Close the prayer by thanking God for his love and care for us.

Keep the paper wads for use in the Story Excursion experience.

(10 minutes)
Big Plans

In this experience, kids will discover that God has a plan for their lives, just as he did for David.

Gather kids and say: **Let's find out more about how** God **loves and watches over us. In the coming weeks, we're going to look at parts of the 23rd Psalm in detail. Today we're going to look at the whole psalm.**

A man named David wrote the 23rd Psalm. David was an important person in the Bible. He was even a relative of Jesus—he lived many years before Jesus, of course. But David didn't start out so important. He started out as a simple shepherd boy, and he ended up being king!

None of the good things in David's life would've happened without God's love and care. It's the same way with us. God loves and watches over us throughout our entire lives.

Right now, you're still young. But God has big plans for your life. The Bible says so. Listen to what the Bible says. Read aloud Jeremiah 29:11. Now think of a dream or hope you have for your life. While you're thinking, I'll pass out supplies.

Give each person a sheet of white paper, a white or light-colored crayon, a dark crayon, and a paper clip.

Say: **Use your light-colored crayon to write a word or draw a picture that shows something good you hope for in your life. Maybe someday you'd like to be a great athlete, a person who works with animals, someone who teaches children, or someone who tells others about God's Word. Or maybe there's something you're hoping for right now, like doing better in school!**

Give kids time to write or draw. When everyone has finished, say: **Now use your dark-colored crayon to color over all of what you just wrote or drew.**

As kids are coloring, say: **Sometimes we face worries and may think God isn't caring for us. David wrote some psalms that asked God to hurry up and protect him or that asked God not to forget him.**

But God never forgot David, and he never forgets us. God is always watching out for us. God loves and watches over us—all the time—even if we can't quite see it. I'll show you what I mean.**

Show kids how to use the edge of a paper clip to scratch away the dark crayon coloring on their paper. What they wrote or drew with the light-colored crayon will reappear.

Say: **Look! Your hope for something good is still there, even when you couldn't see it.**

Ask: • **How is the dark coloring like our problems or worries?**

• **What can we do to help us remember that, no matter what's going on in our lives, God's still watching over us?**

Say: **God's love and care are always with us. Sometimes we get so**

Younger kids may strongly resist coloring over their drawings—reassure them that their drawings won't be lost, and promise the drawings will actually reappear in a cool way.

caught up in our own problems or worries that we don't see God. But ⊕God loves and watches over us in every situation, just as he did for David. Let's find out more about this guy who wrote the 23rd Psalm.

STORY EXCURSION

(20 minutes)
Discovering David
This activity will take kids on a quick tour of David's life, helping them discover how his words in Psalm 23 apply to their lives.

Items to Pack: Bibles, copy of the "Psalm 23 Stations" handout on page 14, paper wads from the Departure Prayer, sticky notes, a basket, markers, yellow construction paper, scissors, tape, 2 pieces of white poster board, blue poster paint

Ahead of time, copy the "Psalm 23 Stations" handout on page 14, and cut apart the instructions for each of the four Travel Stops. Then create the Travel Stops in your room. At each Travel Stop, place the appropriate instructions (face down) and a Bible. Kids will need to add their paper wads from the Departure Prayer. You'll also need to draw a fierce face on one poster board to represent Goliath and paint a blue lake or stream on the other. Set up each Travel Stop as follows:

Travel Stop 1: Close to a wall, place markers and a basket to hold about half the paper wads from the Departure Prayer. On the opposite wall, place something to represent "still water"—such as a large piece of white poster board with a blue lake painted on it.

Travel Stop 2: Place markers and a pad of sticky notes.

Travel Stop 3: In a corner of the room, place markers and the rest of the paper wads. High up on the wall, tape the poster board with the fierce Goliath face drawn on it.

Travel Stop 4: Place yellow construction paper (one sheet per person), markers, scissors, and tape on a flat work surface.

Open your Bible to Psalm 23, and show kids the passage. Say: **David wrote the 23rd Psalm—and a bunch of the other psalms in the Bible, too. I'm not sure when he wrote this psalm, whether he was young or old. But it's a great example of how ⊕ God loves and watches over us, no matter how old we are.**

Form four groups, and assign each group to one of the Travel Stops. Tell kids not to turn over the instructions until you say "go." Say: **At each of these stops, you'll explore a part of Psalm 23 and a part of David's life. You'll have a few minutes at each Travel Stop, and I'll let you know when it's time to move to the next stop. Are you ready? Turn over your instructions and begin!**

TOUR GUIDE TIP

Pretend you don't notice when kids are sticking you with sticky notes. You might want to station yourself at Travel Stop 4 and help kids with the crown-making activity.

Give kids a few minutes at each Travel Stop. When kids have rotated through all four stops, have them sit in a circle with you.

Ask: • **Talk about your favorite Travel Stop.**

• **Tell why you chose to write what you did on your crowns.**

• **What's the favorite thing you learned about David?**

• **How does this help you understand Psalm 23 better?**

• **What feelings did David express in just this one psalm?**

Say: **David expressed many feelings in just this one psalm.** (If kids don't mention the following, mention them also: He acknowledged God for all God provides. He talked about how God guided him in making right decisions. He said that even when he was scared, God was with him. And he said that God not only gave him blessings here on earth, God offered him eternal life, too.)

That's a lot to say in such a short space!

Let's try writing our own psalms.

ADVENTURES IN GROWING

(10 minutes)

My Own Psalm

This experience will help kids discover that Psalm 23 applies directly to them.

Give each person a sheet of paper and a pencil.

Say: **Let's try writing our own psalms to God, using the four parts of David's psalm I've written down. If you need to refresh your memory, feel free to read Psalm 23 as many times as necessary. Mention things from your life in your psalm, just as David did. Your psalm doesn't have to be long, and you won't have to show it to anyone else if you don't want to. Just write about how God helps you in these four areas.**

Give kids time to write, and offer help as needed. When everyone has finished, gather kids. Ask willing kids to share the psalms they wrote.

Ask: • **How can the psalm you wrote help you this week?**

Say: **Psalms are a way of talking to God, which is good to do any time. This week remember what you wrote. Hang your psalm in your room at home, or put it in a school notebook. Let it help you remember that just as God loved and watched over David,** ⬤ **God loves and watches over us**.

Items to Pack: Bibles, paper, pencils, poster board and marker (or chalkboard and chalk)

TOUR GUIDE TIP

Write these four themes of David's psalm on a chalkboard or sheet of poster board for kids to refer to. The parts are (1) God's provision; (2) God's guidance in making right decisions; (3) God's help when we're afraid; and (4) God's blessings and promise of eternal life.

SOUVENIRS →

(10 minutes)

The Lord Is My Shepherd

Kids will begin their Travel Journals and create their first Souvenir.
This experience will help kids see that God, through the Bible, speaks directly to each of us.

Distribute one pocket folder to each child, and have kids write their names on the front. These folders will serve as kids' Travel Journals to collect the Souvenir experience in each lesson. Kids will take their Journals and Souvenirs home after Lesson 13 to remind them about the 23rd Psalm.

Give each person a pen or pencil and a copy of the "The Lord Is My Shepherd" handout.

Say: **God loves and watches over us. To help you understand that for sure, read through Psalm 23 on y our handout. Write your own name on all the blank lines.**

Give kids time to write. When they've finished, ask:

• How does writing your own name in Psalm 23 make it seem different from when you first heard the psalm as David wrote it?

• What's one thing you can do this week to remember how God loves and watches over you?

Say: **Let's thank God right now for his incredible love for us.**

Have kids place their handouts in their Travel Journals.

HOME AGAIN PRAYER

(10 minutes)

Use this experience to reinforce how much God loves kids.

Say: **There are all sorts of ways to talk to God. We can speak to him, write to him as David did, sing to him, and even dance for him. David did that once, but that's a whole different part of the Bible.**

For now, let's combine a few methods as we pray to God. I'll say verses of Psalm 23, adding a motion. Then you'll repeat the words and motions.

Here we go.

Have kids stand in a circle with you. Say Psalm 23 aloud and lead kids in the following motions.

The Lord is my shepherd (*point to self*)**;**
I have all that I need. (*Stretch arms out wide.*)

FUN FACT

In the book of Genesis, many important people were shepherds: Abel, Abraham, Lot, Isaac, and Jacob were all shepherds. The wives of Isaac and Jacob were shepherdesses. And Joseph introduced his family to Pharaoh as shepherds.

He lets me rest in green meadows *(put palms together at one side of face)*;

He leads me beside peaceful streams. *(Make wavelike motions with hands.)*

He renews my strength. *(Make muscles.)*

He guides me along right paths *(walk in place)*,

Bringing honor to his name. *(Point up.)*

Even when I walk through the darkest valley *(cup hands over eyes)*,

I will not be afraid *(hug self)*,

For you are close beside me. *(Point left and right.)*

Your rod and your staff protect and comfort me. *(Cross fists in front of you.)*

You prepare a feast for me in the presence of my enemies. *(Pretend to eat.)*

You honor me by anointing my head with oil. *(Touch hands to head.)*

My cup overflows with blessings. *(Cup hands in front of you.)*

Surely your goodness and unfailing love will pursue me all the days of my life *(turn in a circle)*,

And I will live in the house of the Lord forever. *(Stretch arms up high.)*
Amen.

Psalm 23 Stations

Directions: Cut apart the four sections below, and place each at the appropriate Travel Stop.

Travel Stop 1

Read Psalm 23:1-2 together.

• David was a shepherd boy when he was young.

• Take two of the paper wads, and write one word on each that describes something good God gives you. Then guide your sheep (those paper wads) across the room to the "water" and back—without using your hands.

Travel Stop 2

• Read Psalm 23:3 together.

• One time, after they became enemies, David could have killed Saul, but he knew that wouldn't please God. Instead, he snuck up on Saul and secretly cut off part of his robe.

• Write one word on a sticky note that stands for something you need God's help with. Then take the note, sneak up on your leader, and stick it on his or her back. Don't get caught!

Travel Stop 3

• Read Psalm 23:4 together.

• When David was young, he faced an enemy who was big—really big—like 10 feet tall! He killed this giant, who was called Goliath, using only a few small stones and a slingshot.

• Take two or three of the paper wads, and on each one write one worry or fear that you'd like God to help you with. Then see how many times you can hit Goliath with your paper "stones."

Travel Stop 4

• Read Psalm 23:5-6 together.

• God cared for David, and he took him from being a shepherd boy to being king.

• Your job is to make a kingly crown to wear. On your crown, write the first thing you'd do to bless others if you were king.

The Lord is _____ shepherd;

_____ has all that _____ needs.

He lets _____ rest in green meadows;

he leads _____ beside peaceful streams.

He renews _____ strength.

He guides _____ along right paths,

bringing honor to his name.

Even when _____ walks through the darkest valley,

_____ will not be afraid,

for you are close beside _____ .

Your rod and your staff protect and comfort _____ .

You prepare a feast for _____

in the presence of _____ enemies.

You honor _____ by anointing

_____ head with oil.

_____ cup overflows with blessings.

Surely your goodness and unfailing love will pursue

_____ all the days of _____ life,

and _____ will live in the house of the Lord forever.

(Psalm 23)

JOURNEY 2

All That I Need

Pathway Point:  We belong to God.

In-Focus Verse: "The Lord is my shepherd; I have all that I need" (Psalm 23:1).

Travel Itinerary

One of the most basic needs of the human heart is to belong. The security of belonging in a family gives young children a foundation to explore their world as they grow and develop. As children move through early elementary and into the preteen years, their experience of belonging expands to include other groups. And kids developmentally prepare for adolescence, when they'll become more independent of their families.

Prepare your children for a healthy navigation of these transitions by helping them find their sense of belonging in God's family. Belonging to God secures us as accepted, valued, and loved people, freeing us to love God and serve others.

TOUR GUIDE TIP The experiences in this book have been designed for multi-age groups. Select from the experiences, or adapt them as needed.

Items to Pack: stuffed animal, ribbon, card stock, scissors, pen

DEPARTURE PRAYER (up to 5 minutes)

Ahead of time, create a pet ID tag out of card stock, thread it on a piece of ribbon, and tie it around the stuffed animal's neck as a collar.

Have kids sit in a circle, and show them the stuffed animal with its ribbon collar and ID tag. Briefly lead kids in discussing the responsibilities of caring for a pet and the purpose of pet ID tags.

Then ask: • **Why are pets so important to us?**

• **What are some ways we take good care of our pets?**

Say: • **We take good care of our pets because we love them and they depend on us to keep them safe. If they get lost, we want others to know they belong to our family. We're going to learn that God loves us far more than we love our pets. We can depend on him to care for us and watch over us.**

Ask: • **Why is it important to belong to a family?**

• **What's good about belonging to your family?**

• **Why is it important to belong to God?**

• **What are some ways God takes care of us?**

SCENIC ROUTE → Use a real pet collar and ID tag if you have one.

Say: **Let's go around the circle and each say our name and thank God that we belong to him. I'll begin:**

Pray: **Dear, God, my name is** [your name]. **I'm thankful I belong to you.**

When all the children have prayed, close the prayer, thanking God that you and the children are part of his family and asking him to show you more about the blessings of belonging.

 (15 minutes)
Lost and Found

Ahead of time, make two signs for the box, one "Lost and Found" and the other "Found and Saved!" Attach the Lost and Found sign to the box with tape. (Set aside the Found and Saved! sign for use in the Home Again Prayer.) Gather items for the box. Include enough items for each child to have one.

Say: **Lots of schools and churches have a lost and found box. If people find something out of place and don't know who it belongs to, they put it into a lost and found box. If people lose something, they know to check the lost and found box to see if someone else may've found it.**

Take the box around the circle and have each child choose an item from the box. Then go around the circle, and have each child guess how his or her item may've been lost and how its loss might affect the owner.

Ask: • **What's good about having a lost and found box?**

• **Why are some items never found by their owners?**

• **What do you think should happen to items that are unclaimed?**

Say: **Sometimes owners claim the items in a lost and found box. But often, lost items just stay lost. The owner might give up looking for the lost item. Eventually, someone gives these items to a charity or throws them away.**

The Bible tells us that people are also lost. We want to run our own lives and think we know what's best. And that makes us get lost from God. We go our own way and become separated from God. But because God loves us so much, he doesn't give up on us or leave us in the lost and found box. He comes looking for us.

Ask: • **What are some things people do that show they're going their own way instead of following God?**

Items to Pack: large box (big enough for a child's feet to fit inside so a child can stand up in it); paper; tape; markers; and articles usually found in a lost and found box, such as glasses, hat, small toys, or school items

TOUR GUIDE TIP
Use your church's lost and found box if it has one. Supplement with additional items if needed.

• **What are some ways God shows us that he looks for us?**

Say: **Today we'll read in the Bible about how persistent God is in looking for people who are lost from him. Because of his great love for us, God sent Jesus to find us.**

Have kids return their items to the lost and found box, and set it aside for later use.

STORY EXCURSION
(15 minutes)

Lost Sheep

Kids will play a cotton ball activity to learn about a shepherd's love for one lost sheep and God's love for one lost person.

Gather children around a table and bring out the cotton balls. Say: **We talked earlier about pets wearing ID tags in case they got lost. Our pets are so important to us that if they get lost, it causes a lot of worry until they're found. People work very hard to find lost pets.** Invite one or two children to briefly share their experiences with lost pets.

Then have kids count the cotton balls into 10 piles of 10—for a total of 100 cotton balls. While kids are counting, place 10 paper cups upside-down on the table.

Say: **Suppose you had 100 cotton balls and lost one.** Remove one cotton ball. **Would you worry about it? Probably not.** Return the cotton ball. **Now suppose that each one of these cotton balls was a sheep. What if one of them got lost?** Place one cotton ball underneath one of the cups, and shuffle all the cups until kids lose track of which cup hides the cotton ball. **Would you do anything about it? That depends on what kind of shepherd you are. If you're just a worker who doesn't care much for the sheep, it might not seem like a big deal. One hundred sheep all in a pen look like a lot of sheep. You might not even notice one was missing. But if you're a good shepherd, each one would be important, and you'd probably spend a lot of time looking for the one that was gone.**

Have kids guess how many cups they'll have to turn over until the cotton ball is found. Then invite kids, one at a time, to turn over a cup until it's found.

Say: **Jesus tells a story about being lost and found; it's in Luke's Gospel.** Open your Bible and read aloud Luke 15:3-7.

Say: **One cotton ball isn't very important, and some may think one sheep isn't very important either. But it was important to this shepherd.**

Items to Pack: Bible, cotton balls, small paper cups

FUN FACT

There are 150 yards (450 feet) of sheep's wool in a baseball!

• Ask: **What did Jesus say makes someone a good shepherd?**

• **What did Jesus want us to know about God?**

God loves us—much more than an earthly shepherd loves his sheep. He loves us so much that he gave his own son to find us. Jesus came to earth, did many miracles, and taught people about God. But most important, he died on the cross so our sins could be forgiven and we could be brought back to God's family. Because we believe Jesus died for us, ●we belong to God.

Have children form pairs, and give each pair 10 cotton balls and three cups to play the hidden cotton ball game with each other. Each time kids uncover the cotton ball, have them name a person they know who's been found by Jesus.

Ask: • **What does it tell you about God to know how much he wants to find all of us?**

• **How can God use you to find others and bring them back to God?**

Say: **In the Bible, the shepherd was so happy to find his lost sheep that he called all his friends to share his good news and to celebrate. Jesus says heaven is full of joy whenever a lost person comes back to God.**

(up to 10 minutes)
Blessings of Belonging

Kids will discover that even in difficult situations they can find peace in remembering they belong to God.

Say: **Today's verse from the 23rd Psalm says, "The Lord is my Shepherd; I have all that I need" (Psalm 23:1). We've learned that because Jesus is the Good Shepherd, he searched for us when we were lost and now ●we belong to God. Just as sheep need to be part of a flock where they'll be safe and cared for, people also need a group where they're loved and cared for. Our families and friends do this for us, but sometimes even our families or friends may let us down or make us feel left out.**

Ask: • **When have you felt left out or like you didn't belong?**

• **How can it help to remember that ●we belong to God at times like that?**

Then read the following vignettes, and after each one ask these questions:

SCENIC ROUTE →
Have kids brainstorm the groups they belong to—church, sports teams, school classes, scouting or 4-H, music or dance groups, and so on—and ask them what they enjoy about belonging to these groups.

• How would you feel in this situation?

• How could you help this person who feels left out or lonely?

Vignette 1: Gretchen's family moved to a new city, and today's her first day at a new school.

Vignette 2: Trevor found out that several good friends were invited to another friend's birthday party, but he wasn't.

Vignette 3: Kelsey's church is having a father-daughter dance, but Kelsey's parents are divorced and her dad lives too far away to come.

Vignette 4: Sam found out that his two best friends are on the same soccer team, but he's on a different team with kids he's never met.

Ask: • **When you're feeling left out and alone, how will you remind yourself that  you belong to God?**

• What's one thing you can do this week to remind someone that he or she belongs to God?

Say: **No matter what age you are, no matter where you go, no matter what challenges your family faces, no matter how your friends treat you, you can always know that you belong to God. Belonging to Jesus is the most important relationship you'll ever have. When you feel alone or left out, you can know that with Jesus as your shepherd and as part of God's family, there'll always be others you can turn to for help.**

SOUVENIRS → (10 minutes)
Bag Tags
Kids will create a bag tag to remind them that they can find their "ID" in God.

Items to Pack: copies of the "Bag Tag" handout on page 22, scissors, markers, sample tag, backpack or duffel bag, stapler

Say: **When you go on a journey, you usually take a suitcase or bag to carry your belongings. People often have tags on their luggage to identify the owner. Today we're going to make tags that will not only tell who the bag belongs to, they'll also tell who *we* belong to.**

Give each child a copy of the handout. Read through the tag's verse with children, and have them cut out the outlined tag. Show them where to fill in their names on both sides of the tags, and encourage them to decorate the tags with markers. As children work, circulate among them and invite children to read their tags to you with their names inserted. As kids finish, show a sample tag and how it can be placed through the strap of a bag and then stapled in place.

Ask: • **How can others tell that you belong to God?**

• **How could this tag help someone else learn about belonging to God?**

Have children fold the tags and place them in their Travel Journals.

HOME AGAIN PRAYER (10 minutes)

Have kids join hands and stand in a circle. Place the empty "Lost and Found" box in the center of the circle.

Say: **Today we learned that although all people are lost in sin, God doesn't want us to stay lost. He comes to find us, just as the shepherd looked for his lost sheep. God calls us when we hear his Word in church, when we read the Bible, and when others tell us about Jesus. When we trust in Jesus, we belong to God and are part of his family. Being found by Jesus is like getting rescued out of the lost and found box** (indicate the sign on the box) **and moved into a new box—God's "Found and Saved!" box.** Bring out the sign reading "Found and Saved! and tape it over the "Lost and Found" sign. Show the box to the entire circle.

To close in prayer, have children step into the box, one at a time, and pray, "Thank you God for finding and saving me. I belong to you." Have the children clap and cheer for each "found" member of the group.

SCENIC ROUTE → If you'd like to make kids' souvenirs a little sturdier, copy the reproducible page onto card stock. If you have younger kids, have them embellish their tags by gluing on a cotton ball and adding a head, tail, legs or other details.

Items to Pack: empty box from the "Lost and Found" activity, tape, a sign reading "Found and Saved!"

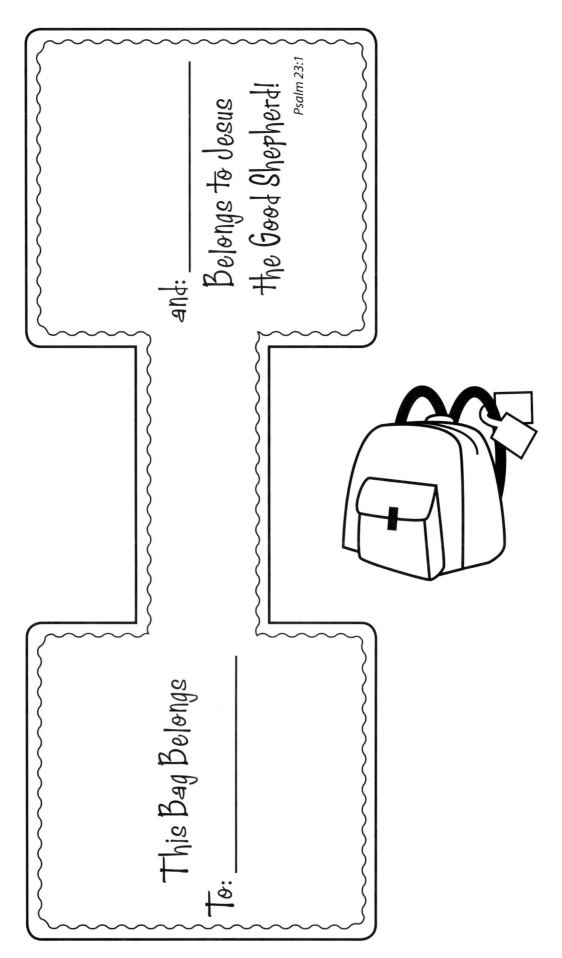

and: _____

Belongs to Jesus
the Good Shepherd!

Psalm 23:1

This Bag Belongs

To: _____

At Rest in Green Meadows

Pathway Point: ◐ We're in God's care.

In-Focus Verse: "He lets me rest in green meadows" (Psalm 23:2a).

Travel Itinerary

Imagine your favorite spot to relax. Is it lying on a sunny beach, listening to the soothing sound of ocean waves? Sitting in the cool shade of a wind-rustled tree after an invigorating hike up a mountain trail? Perhaps it's snuggling under a quilt with a cup of cocoa while snowflakes drift lazily outside the window. What is it that draws us to these images with a soothing sigh? It's probably the promise of rest that leaves worries and demands behind.

Given the driven nature of our society, rest has become an elusive wish rather than a regular part of our lives. Today Jesus invites you to rest and to create an experience of rest for the children in your ministry. Even at their young age, children may already be as weary and rest-hungry as their parents and teachers. Use this week's experience to reconnect yourself and your children with the Good Shepherd who calls us to come and rest.

TOUR GUIDE TIP The experiences in this book have been designed for multi-age groups. Select from the experiences, or adapt them as needed.

Items to Pack: box; rocks of various sizes, shapes, and colors, 1 per child

| **DEPARTURE PRAYER** | (up to 5 minutes) |

Have kids sit in a circle. Put a box of rocks beside you.

Say: **Usually when we think of rest, we think of sleeping at night or taking a nap. There is, however, another kind of rest we need—rest from our worries. Worry is the uncomfortable feeling we have when we think about troubles but don't know what to do about them. Think about one of the worries you have right now.**

Ask: • **If this worry was a rock, how big would it be? how sharp or smooth?**

Say: **Now come over to the box of rocks, and pick out one rock that reminds you of something you worry about. You won't have to tell anyone what it is.** Have kids each pick out a rock.

When we worry, we think over and over about our problems or bad things we're afraid may happen. Worrying makes it hard to think about anything else. When we worry, we can't feel peaceful or happy.

TOUR GUIDE TIP Take a moment to rest at a nearby stream or lake and gather rocks. No time to rest? Rocks are also available by the bag in craft stores!

TOUR GUIDE TIP

Be sensitive to worries expressed by your children, especially those who have serious family concerns. God often cares for children by alerting caring adults to situations kids can't handle by themselves. If you're concerned about a child's physical or emotional well-being, involve your pastor or children's minister in following up. If you suspect child abuse, you're required by law to report it. Requirements vary by state.

Items to Pack: tote bag, 4 or 5 large rocks

TOUR GUIDE TIP

If you don't have access to large rocks, use bricks instead. If kids have many worries to share, repeat the experience so everyone has a chance to hold the heavy load.

Ask: • **What does being really worried about something do to the way your body feels? your mind?**

• **When you feel worried, what do you do to feel better?**

Say: **Because we belong to God, he provides for all our needs—and that includes rest from our worries. God doesn't want us to carry our worries around with us. God invites us to bring all our worries to him and know that we don't need to worry because** **we're in God's care.**

Say: **Now hold your rock in your hands and think of this one thing you're worried about while we pray:**

Pray: **Dear God, thank you for letting us know we can always come to you whenever we feel worried. Help us find rest and peace in you. In Jesus' name. Amen.**

Gather the rocks and set them aside to use later in the Home Again Prayer.

1st STOP DISCOVERY (15 minutes)

Worry Is a Heavy Load

Kids will explore how worries weigh us down.

Say: **Some people worry more than others. Something that worries one person may not worry someone else. Let's think about the different worries people have.**

Ask: • **What do kids worry about?**

• **What do you think grown-ups worry about?**

Say: **Sometimes worries make us feel weary, like we're carrying a heavy load. Imagine you had to carry a heavy rock for each thing you worried about.**

Invite a child to hold the tote bag and share something he or she worries about. Add one large rock to the bag. Then invite a second child to take the bag, share another worry, and add another rock to the bag. Continue to pass the bag to other kids until all the rocks have been added to the bag.

After all the kids have had a turn holding the bag full of heavy rocks, ask:

• **How would you feel if you knew you had to keep carrying this bag, all day, every day?**

• **What would be the biggest challenge during an ordinary day if you had to carry this bag everywhere?**

Say: **Today's verse from the 23rd Psalm tells us, "[The Good Shepherd] lets us rest in green meadows." That means** **we're in God's care. We don't have to be weighed down by our worries. Jesus invites us to set our worries down and rest.**

STORY EXCURSION

(15 minutes)

Look at the Birds!

Kids will work together to create birds or flowers while considering God's generous care for all his creation.

Items to Pack: Bible, plastic foam cups, white paper, scissors, glue sticks, colorful craft feathers, chenille stems, a variety of colored paper, colored markers

Have kids form groups of three, and give each group one plastic foam cup, one sheet of white paper, scissors, glue sticks, and colored markers. Then give craft feathers to half the groups, and instruct them to create a bird. Give the other groups chenille stems and colored paper. Instruct those groups to create a flower. Allow about five minutes for kids to work. When children are finished, have them share their creations with the other groups.

Say: **These are wonderful creations—each one unique and beautiful. Not only did God create birds and flowers to be beautiful and to grow and reproduce, but he also provides for all their needs day by day.**

In today's Scripture, Jesus encourages us to look at birds and flowers not just to enjoy their beauty but also to learn something from them. Read aloud Matthew 6:25-34.

Ask: • **What sorts of worries do all people experience?**

• **Why do you think people worry so much if it doesn't change anything?**

• **Why does Jesus tell us we don't have to worry?**

Say: **As much as God loves the beautiful birds and flowers he's created, the Bible tells us that we're much more valuable to God than birds and flowers. So we, too, can trust him to give us what we need. Instead of worrying, Jesus wants us to trust him. Even when troubles come, Jesus is with us and will help us face whatever challenges we encounter.**

Ask: • **How is trusting Jesus a way to find rest?**

• **When you feel worried, why is it better to trust Jesus than to keep on carrying your worries around?**

SCENIC ROUTE → Use leftover wrapping paper or wallpaper remnants to give kids more options for their creations.

FUN FACT What do kids worry about? In a KidsHealth.org poll, top worries among ages 9-13 were about the health of a loved one (55%), the future (43%), schoolwork (37%), looks or appearance (37%), and making mistakes (26%). Other top worriers for kids: war or terrorism, friends and their problems, and the environment.

Items to Pack: images of items and people that represent God's care for us: clothes, food, school books, bike helmet, cross, Bible, box of bandages, toys, families, friends, and churches

ADVENTURES IN GROWING

(up to 10 minutes)

God's Care Packages

Kids will choose images that reflect God's visible and invisible care.

In this experience, kids will discover ways God responds to their worries and provides for them. Some problems and worries children face don't lend themselves to simple, object-lesson answers. Jesus himself told us as much when he said, "Here on earth you will have many trials and sorrows." Yet he continued, "But take heart, because I have overcome the world" (John 16:33). Lead kids to connect to the one who's overcome, so they'll find strength in trusting Jesus to care for them through tough times.

Have kids sit in a circle around the images you've collected.

Say: **Because we're even more valuable to God than birds and flowers, we know we're in God's care.**

Let's look at some things that can remind us of the many ways God cares for us. The items shown here don't represent all the ways God cares for us. Some of God's care is visible, like clothes and food, but some is *invisible,* like the love of our families or the way God has created our bodies to grow and to heal when we're sick or injured. Whether his care is visible or invisible, God is the provider of all that we need.

TOUR GUIDE TIP

If you're in contact with your children's families during the week, ask them to bring in nonperishable foods. Then donate their items to a food pantry for those in need. Tell children that God can use us to provide for other people's needs.

Have each child choose one item from the collection of photos and share with the group how it shows God's care. If you have more than eight children, form smaller groups before sharing.

Say: **While some of God's "care packages" are easy to see, such as food on our tables and homes that keep us safe and dry, sometimes God's care comes in packages we can't see. For example, God gives us strength to keep trying even if schoolwork is hard. When we worry about someone who's sick, God gives us peace by letting us know that person is in his care.**

SCENIC ROUTE

If you want, you can bring in a collection of actual items for this experience, instead of cutting out photos.

Ask: • **What are some other invisible ways God cares for us?**

• **How does it help us rest to know that we're in God's care?**

SOUVENIRS

(10 minutes)

Leave Worries With Jesus

Kids will create a picture to remind them to leave their worries with Jesus and rest in his care.

Items to Pack: copies of the "Leave Worries With Jesus" handout on page 29, markers

Give each child a copy of the handout. To the left of the picture of Jesus, have kids draw something they worry about. Next have kids fold the left side of the picture toward the middle on the dotted line. Then on the left side of the picture, have kids draw themselves in a peaceful place. While kids work, read the verse at the top, "Give all your worries and cares to God, for he cares about you" (1 Peter 5:7).

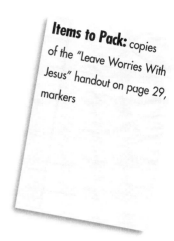

Ask: • **What's your favorite place to go when you want to feel peaceful?**

• **What can we do if worries begin to bother us again?**

• **What will Jesus do about the worries we've left with him?**

Say: **When we're worried, it's hard to feel peaceful and calm. But when we pray and leave our worries with Jesus, we can remember that we're in God's care. Just as God cares for birds and flowers, he promises to care for us because he loves us so much. Leaving our cares with Jesus lets us feel rested and at peace.**

Have children place their handouts in their Travel Journals.

HOME AGAIN PRAYER

(10 minutes)

Have children sit in a circle. Place the cross on the floor in the center of the circle. Give each child a rock.

Say: **Today we learned we're in God's care. Just as God cares for plants and animals in creation, God has promised he'll provide for us. Because God keeps his promises, we can rest in his care. Hold your rock in your hands as you look at the cross and think about Jesus.** (Pause.) **Jesus showed his love for us by dying on the cross to forgive our sins. When he came back to life, he showed he has power over all the things that worry us. He can help us in any situation because we're in his care.**

As we pray, let's leave our worries with Jesus and rest in his care. As you lay your rock by the cross, pray silently about whatever worries you, and ask Jesus to give you his peace. Pause and allow several children at a time to bring their rocks to the cross. They can then return to their

Items to Pack: Bible, 2 rolls of blue crepe paper streamers, masking tape, towel, a picture of a child

FUN FACT

The bones of most birds are hollow and filled with air. This enables their skeletons to be strong, yet light enough to fly. In fact, a pigeon's feathers weigh more than its bones!

place in the circle. Continue until all have had a turn. **Now close your eyes and imagine being in a peaceful green meadow with Jesus.**

Pray: **Dear Jesus, thank you for keeping us in your care. Thank you for teaching us what to do when we feel worried. When we see birds or flowers, remind us ◐ we're in your care. Help us leave our worries with you and trust you to provide for us and give us rest. In your name. Amen.**

"Give all your worries and cares to God, for he cares about you." 1 Peter 5:7

Beside Peaceful Streams

Pathway Point: God asks us to trust and follow.

In-Focus Verse: "He leads me beside peaceful streams" (Psalm 23:2b).

Travel Itinerary

Jesus frequently used sheep and shepherds as object lessons to help people recognize that like sheep, they're dependent creatures, lost and in need of God's care. He also wanted people to understand he wasn't like other spiritual shepherds they'd know—shepherds who'd exploited the flock and then deserted it in times of danger.

Jesus is different. Here's a shepherd whose first priority is the sheep—us. As children experience Jesus' love and acceptance in your ministry, at church, and in their families, they'll grow to trust him and recognize his voice. This trusting relationship is the only basis for a command to follow. Demands to follow that are based on rules and laws are the voice of a stranger. Children (and adults) won't follow very long. But when a child's vulnerable heart experiences the protecting, comforting, self-sacrificing love of the Good Shepherd, following after such love becomes the natural response.

TOUR GUIDE TIP The experiences in this book have been designed for multi-age groups. Select from the experiences, or adapt them as needed.

Items to Pack: large bowl, large pitcher of water

SCENIC ROUTE → Use a small fountain for this experience if you have access to one. They're also available at discount and hardware stores. You'll use this again for the Home Again Prayer.

DEPARTURE PRAYER (up to 5 minutes)

Ahead of time, set up the bowl and pitcher of water where children won't see them but will be able to hear the water being poured when they're quiet.

Gather kids and say: **Because we're on a journey learning about the 23rd Psalm, let's think about places you might begin a long journey. If you travel by bus, you might start at a bus station. Everyone make sounds like you'd hear on a bus.** Pause and allow kids to make noises. **Or you might begin at an airport. Everyone make sounds like you'd hear at an airport.** Pause while kids make noises. Raise your voice over the noise to regain kids' attention; then quickly reduce your voice to a whisper. Have a helper begin pouring the water into the bowl.

Say: **Sometimes places are so noisy that we miss hearing quieter things. Let's get as quiet as possible and listen for what we can hear.** Pause and allow children to listen and identify the sound of water. Then show children the water being poured into the bowl. **Let's close our eyes and listen for a bit. Notice how the sound makes you feel.** Allow children to listen quietly for a few moments.

Ask: • **Where else have you heard quiet sounds of water?**

• **What other sounds give you a quiet, peaceful feeling?**

Say: **No matter how noisy or busy our lives get, we can have this quiet, peaceful feeling any time we meet with Jesus and talk to him. Our verse today from the 23rd Psalm says, "He leads me beside peaceful streams" (Psalm 23:2b). Let's get quiet as if we're sitting by a peaceful stream and talk with Jesus now.**

Pray: **Dear Jesus, we know that we belong to you and you care for us. Thank you for giving us peaceful times like this when we can talk with you. Help us listen when ◔ you ask us to trust and follow. Amen.**

Have your helper empty the bowl and refill the pitcher, and then set them out of the way until the Home Again Prayer.

 (15 minutes)
Who's Calling?

Kids will sharpen their listening skills and discover their ability to recognize the sounds they hear.

Arrange beforehand for two parents of children in your room to help with this experience. Ask them to keep their participation a surprise for their children. They'll wait out of sight and when cued, they'll take turns calling their children's names. You'll also need another person stationed out of sight to help with sound effects.

Say: **We're going to do a listening experiment. I have a helper waiting out of sight. When my helper makes a sound, see if you can guess what the sound is.**

Cue your helper to make the following sounds, allowing time for children to listen and guess each sound. First have your helper ring the bell. Next have your helper jingle the bag of coins. Finally, have your helper cue the two parents, one by one, to call their children's names. Help children identify whose parents are calling, and then invite the parents to join the group for the discussion.

Ask: • **How did these children know it was their parents' voices?**

• **Tell about a time you heard your parents call your name.**

• **Why do we feel differently when we hear our parents call our name than if a stranger calls our name?**

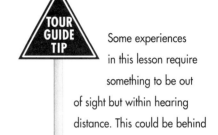

Some experiences in this lesson require something to be out of sight but within hearing distance. This could be behind a room divider or outside the door to your room.

Items to Pack: a bell, coins in a small bag

Children may be very excited to have a parent join them. Use this to illustrate the joy Christians have in recognizing Jesus' voice as he calls us to follow him.

Say: **Just as we learn to recognize and trust our parents' voices, we can learn to recognize Jesus' voice when he calls us, too. Jesus speaks to us through the Bible and through those who know Jesus and teach us about him. Today we're going to listen to Jesus speak to us through something he told his disciples.**

STORY EXCURSION (15 minutes)

The Shepherd's Gate

Children will work in groups to discover the security of being part of God's flock.

Items to Pack: Bibles, large poster board, whiteboard or newsprint, markers

Ahead of time, draw a cross on the poster board, which you'll use for a gate. On a whiteboard or newsprint, write the two questions kids will answer: "What dangers do the sheep face?" and "How does the Good Shepherd protect the sheep?"

Set up the poster board to serve as a gate in the middle of the room. Stabilize the gate between chairs, and when it's time for the children to pass through, have a helper raise the gate. On one side of the room, use chairs to form a circular "sheep pen" that's big enough for all the children to fit inside. The opposite area of the room, on the other side of the gate, will serve as the pasture.

Form two groups near the gate, outside the pen. Provide each group with Bibles to share, and explain the layout of the room.

Say: **Our two groups are going to represent two flocks of sheep, one in the sheep pen and one out in the pasture. Each group will read part of our Bible passage and answer two questions: "What dangers do the sheep face?" and "How does the Good Shepherd protect the sheep?"** Show the questions on the board or newsprint. **When your group has read the story and answered the questions, think of a way to act it out.**

Lead the first group into the sheep pen. Tell them to read John 10:1-10. Gather the second group in the pasture, and tell them to read John 10:11-16, 27-29. Give children time to work, and then have each group share the answers they've discovered and act out their portion of the Bible account.

Say: **By telling this story about sheep, Jesus wanted people to understand that they, like the sheep, were lost and separated from God. Jesus wanted them to recognize the dangers so they'd ◑ trust and follow him.**

SCENIC ROUTE → Talk about people in the Bible who heard God speak in an audible voice: Moses at the burning bush (Exodus 3-4); Samuel, as he fell asleep (1 Samuel 3: 1-21); Paul, at his conversion (Acts 9:1-9); and Ananias, whom God sent to pray for Paul (Acts 9:10-19).

We, too, are like sheep in Jesus' flock. And Jesus, our good shepherd, gave his life for us. He died on the cross so our sins would be forgiven. As his sheep, we recognize our Shepherd's voice and 🌓 trust and follow him. Because he's stronger than all our enemies, no one can snatch us away from him.

Ask: • What does Jesus mean when he says he has other sheep that aren't in his sheep pen?

• What would you say to your friends to encourage them to trust Jesus?

Say: When we look at a large flock of sheep, it's hard to tell one from another. They all look alike. But we're not just a bunch of people to Jesus. The Bible says that Jesus knows each of us by name. Let's call the name of each person who's part of the flock inside the sheep pen. As you hear your name, come out through the gate, choose a partner in the other flock, and tell your partner why you trust Jesus and follow him.

Call children's names one by one until all have found a partner. Form one trio if you have an uneven number of children. When everyone has a partner, have pairs return to the sheep pen through the gate. Join the children inside the sheep pen, and then open your Bible and read aloud John 10:27-29.

Say: One of the best things about belonging to God's flock is Jesus' promise of eternal life. Someday we'll live forever in heaven with Jesus, where there'll be no troubles, dangers, or worries. When 🌓 God asks us to trust and follow, we have his promise that no one can snatch us away from him.

TOUR GUIDE TIP If the first group doesn't talk about Jesus being the gate for the sheep, take time to point out the cross on the gate, and tell children that Jesus is the only way for anyone to be forgiven and become part of God's family.

FUN FACT Not-So-Fun Fact: Even inside the sheep pen, sheep were still vulnerable to attack by robbers who would at times climb over the wall, kill as many animals as possible, and fling the bodies over the wall to other thieves waiting outside. We aren't as vulnerable as sheep, though—Jesus says no one can snatch us out of God's hands (John 10:28).

ADVENTURES IN GROWING

(up to 10 minutes)
Following the Shepherd
Kids will travel along a peaceful "stream" and discover ways to follow Jesus.

Lay the two blue streamers parallel in a winding path around the room, attaching them to the floor with masking tape. This will represent the stream the children will follow in discovering what it means to trust and follow Jesus. Designate two stopping places along the way and a third stop at the end of the "stream." Place a Bible at the first stop, a towel at the second stop, and a picture of a child at the end.

Gather kids at the beginning of the stream.

Say: 🌓 God asks us to trust and follow him. Today we'll travel

Items to Pack: Bible, 2 rolls of blue crepe paper streamers, masking tape, towel, a picture of a child

In Bible times, several flocks were sometimes allowed to mix, such as when being watered. When it was time to go their separate ways, each shepherd would call his own flock. Sheep would lift their heads and each begin moving toward the call of the shepherd whose voice they recognized, eventually sorting themselves into separate flocks again.

along a peaceful stream to discover what it means to follow Jesus. Each time we come to a rest stop, we'll learn something new. We trust that Jesus loves us and will lead us in ways that are best for us. Begin walking with the children along the route marked by the streamers. Stop at the rest stop marked by the Bible. Hold the Bible and have kids sit with you next to the stream. Lead the following discussion.

Say: **Our first rest stop in following Jesus is "learning." As we learn about Jesus, we come to trust his love for us. As we experience his love, we want to go where Jesus leads us so we can experience more of his love.**

Ask: • **What are some ways we can learn about Jesus?**

• **What have you already learned about Jesus?**

• **Of all the things you've learned about Jesus, what is most important to you?**

Say: **Let's follow along our peaceful stream. Sometimes, as we're following a leader, we don't always know where we're going next. But because we trust Jesus and his love, we can follow with confidence—we know he has good plans for us.** Continue until you come to the towel.

Have the children sit with you.

Say: **This rest stop is "serving." I've put this towel here because it reminds me of when Jesus washed his disciples' feet. Washing feet was a job for someone unimportant, but even though Jesus was most important, he did it to show his followers that serving is the way to express our love for others and for God.**

Ask: • **What are some ways Jesus served others?**

• **How can you serve others?**

• **What are some new ways of serving that you might like to try in the future?**

Continue along the river to the end where the picture of the child is displayed.

Say: **Our last rest stop is "sharing." I put a picture of a child here because as followers of Jesus we have much to share with others. When we share even simple things with others because we follow Jesus, it's important to him.**

Ask: • **Tell about a time you shared something with someone else. How did it affect your relationship with that person?**

• **What are some things that can't be touched that we might share with others?**

Say: **One of the best things we can share with others is our faith. When we tell others about Jesus, we help them understand how much he loves them. We can invite them to be sheep in the Good Shepherd's flock. Whether it's by learning, serving, or sharing,** **God asks us to trust and follow.**

 (10 minutes)

Peaceful Streams

Kids will create a peaceful stream picture to remind them of the different steps in following Jesus.

Items to Pack: copies of the "Peaceful Streams" handout on page 37, chenille wires, glue sticks, assorted markers, pens

Give each child a copy of the handout. Have kids mark three rest stops by drawing a Bible, a towel, and a picture of a friend along the stream. Then children can decorate the rest of the scene by bending chenille wires into various animal or flower shapes and gluing them in place.

Ask: • **When do you feel most peaceful following Jesus?**

• **What are some other voices that might try to call us away from following Jesus?**

• **What are some tough situations when trusting Jesus could bring you peace?**

As children finish, set their pictures aside for the glue to dry, and then place the completed projects in their Travel Journals.

SCENIC ROUTE Younger children can decorate the scene by gluing on cotton balls to make sheep and then using pens or markers to add details.

HOME AGAIN PRAYER (10 minutes)

Bring the pitcher of water, the bowl, and a hand towel, and have children sit in a circle with you. Signal kids to get quiet, close their eyes, and listen to the sound of the water as you slowly pour some of it into the bowl.

Say: **Today we learned** **God asks us to trust and follow. Because Jesus is our Good Shepherd who loves us, we know that he'll always care for us and lead us in ways that are best for us.**

Next I want you to think about something you're thankful for as you follow Jesus. Then come over to me one at a time and place your hands above the bowl so I can pour water over them while I say a prayer for you.

Items to Pack: large bowl, large pitcher of water, hand towel

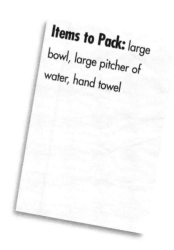

As each child comes forward, pour a bit of water and pray for each one individually.

Pray: **Dear Jesus, may** [child's name]**, always follow you by peaceful streams. In your name. Amen.**

"He leads me beside peaceful streams"

Psalm 23:2b

"I trust and follow Jesus"

JOURNEY 5

New Strength

Pathway Point:  God's power makes us strong.

In-Focus Verse: "He renews my strength" (Psalm 23:3a).

Travel Itinerary

Childhood can be an amazing time—there's a sense of wonder about even the smallest discovery. We all want our children to grow up unaffected by the world's troubles—able to play, laugh, learn, and grow strong. But the world isn't a perfect place: a child's life can be so easily marred. Divorce, poverty, disease, war...children are the smallest and most vulnerable victims of the world's evils. Even in safe, happy, healthy homes, we can't protect children from pain—from a bad grade to the death of a friend or family member. But we worship a God of hope, who renews our strength in the midst of the greatest pain. Help children understand that they can turn to God even during the hardest times of life. Though pain is a given in this world, God can renew our strength in all circumstances. If children learn to look to God for their hope at a young age, they'll continue to do so as they grow older. They'll learn that God—not wealth, circumstances, or even other people—is their source of true strength.

> **TOUR GUIDE TIP**
>
> The experiences in this book have been designed for multi-age groups. Select from the experiences, or adapt them as needed.

Items to Pack: pitcher of water, paper cups, fast-paced worship CD, CD player

> **DEPARTURE PRAYER**

(up to 5 minutes)

Ahead of time, fill a pitcher with water, and set out enough paper cups for each child.

Have kids stand in a circle. Then ask: **Tell about a time you've been really, really tired.** Listen to responses. Then tell kids that they're going to do some exercising right now. Have kids start doing jumping jacks. Play energetic worship music in the background. Have kids do the jumping jacks for about two minutes—until they look pretty tired. Then have kids stop and sit down.

Say: **We tire out our bodies when we exercise and work hard without taking rests.**

Ask: • **What makes you feel better after exercising?**

Say: **Water, food, and rest can all make us feel better when we're physically tired.** Pour cups of water, and pass them around the circle so each child has a cup. **But our bodies aren't the only things that get tired and** need to be rejuvenated. Our minds and our hearts can also get worn out. They get tired when we're stressed out, when we feel pain, when we have fights with other people, or when we experience other hard things.

Ask: • **When have you felt tired in your mind or your heart? What caused you to be tired?**

• **If water, food, and rest help us feel stronger when we're physically tired, what helps us feel better when we're tired in our minds or hearts?**

Say: **It's not as easy to strengthen our hearts and our minds—it takes more than just water or food. But God loves us and he wants us to feel better when we're hurt or tired. God renews our strength and** **God's power makes us strong. We're going to pray now and ask God to renew us and make us strong whenever we're tired or hurting.**

As you pray, have kids take sips of their water whenever you say the word "strong."

Pray: **Dear God, thank you for your power. We know that your power makes us strong. We pray that you'll be with us whenever we're feeling tired or hurt in our minds and hearts. We know that in those times, you're with us and your power makes us strong. Thank you for renewing us and making us strong again. In Jesus' name. Amen.**

 **(10 minutes) Feeling Low**

Children will respond to scenarios that might cause pain or emotional stress.

Have kids stand up and face you.

Say: **We've been learning that the Lord watches over us, guides us, and gives us peace. Psalm 23 tells us that** **God's power also makes us strong. The 23rd Psalm says, "[The Lord] renews my strength." Renew means to make new again—to restore something to what it used to be. So if God "renews" your strength, that means he makes you as strong as you were before you got tired. Imagine if you ran for miles and miles and miles, and you were so tired you couldn't possibly run any farther. If God renewed your strength right then, it would mean you could run miles and miles and miles again...as if you'd never run in the first place.**

But this verse isn't just talking about physical strength; this verse is also talking about our emotional and mental strength. God can renew that as well.

Ask: • **What are some things that make you feel sad or troubled?** Listen to responses.

Say: **I'm going to list some events that might make you feel low or sad. After I say an event, show me just how "low" that event would make you feel. For example, if I said, "It's Christmas morning and you got exactly what you wanted!" That would probably make you feel super-happy, so you would jump up and down. But if I said that you got a bad grade on an important test, that would make you feel pretty bad, so you would duck down kind of low. The sadder an event would make you feel, the lower you squat...if you can't image being sadder, lie down on the floor.**

Read the following list, and give kids time after each one to show how low they'd feel.

• **You miss an important goal playing soccer, and your team loses the game.**

• **You have a fight with your best friend.**

• **You climb a tree, fall off a branch, and break your arm.**

• **You get in trouble for lying to your parents.**

• **Your dog runs away, and you can't find her anywhere.**

Ask: • **What do you do when you feel sad or low? What makes you feel better?**

• **How do you encourage other people when they feel low?**

• **How does God help us when we're feeling sad or low?**

Say: **Life isn't always good or easy; sometimes really painful things happen to us that hurt us and make us sad. Other times, we have a bad day or week or month, and we just get run-down in our minds and hearts. During those really hard times, God never leaves us. He makes us feel better with his words and his presence. He encourages us by putting people in our lives who love and care for us. He reminds us that he loves us. Because we have God in our hearts and minds, we have his power in our lives. And ☽God's power makes us strong. Let's look into the Bible to learn more about this.**

You can come up with more "sad" events if you think of others that might be more appropriate for your group of children. You'll also want to be sensitive to real-life events that have happened to kids in your ministry, such as divorce, sickness, or death. Kids may bring those events up during the discussion time; remind them that God is real and can give them hope during those hard times.

STORY EXCURSION

(15 minutes)

God's Promise

Children will move through the Bible and experience the renewal Jesus offered his disciples.

Items to Pack: Bible; red and orange construction paper; scissors; 2 bedsheets, each with ends tied together to make a "net"; heavy objects like books, weights, or toy blocks; fish-shaped crackers

Set up two different stations ahead of time. At the first station, make a "boat" by lining up chairs to create a boat shape, leaving the middle space open. On one side of the boat, place an empty "fishing net." On the other side of the boat, place a full "fishing net." Use heavy objects to make the net full: books, weights, toy blocks, and other heavy items. At the second station, make a fire by using rocks or toy blocks to create a fire ring and cutting red and orange construction paper flames to set in the center of the ring. Place fish-shaped crackers near the fire.

Turn off or dim the lights; then have kids climb into the boat with you. Encourage kids to rock back and forth with you as if they were on a boat in the waves.

Open your Bible to John 21.

Say: **Today's Scripture comes from the book of John and tells about Jesus and his disciples. Let's close our eyes and imagine we're back there with the disciples.**

Jesus had been killed just a few days ago. The disciples are still grieving and sad about Jesus' death. But also, miraculously, it seems Jesus has come back to life. Many of the disciples have seen him alive again—yet they still aren't exactly sure what to think about everything. Why did Jesus die in the first place? Why hasn't he appeared in full glory to show the Romans and their other enemies that he's alive again? These are the questions going through their minds. And many of them are feeling guilty. They had run away from Jesus and betrayed him when he needed them most. They keep asking themselves why they weren't braver, why they didn't try to save him. They're tired and grieving; their hearts and minds are worn out.

So they decide to go fishing. Many of them were fishermen before they met Jesus, and it seems like the only thing they can think of to do.

Go ahead and open your eyes, and let's see if we can catch some fish. Have kids pull up the empty net and then throw it back and try again. Encourage kids to keep trying, even though they keep coming up empty.

Say: **The disciples kept fishing all through the night. Throwing**

SCENIC ROUTE → Instead of using bedsheets, you can purchase very inexpensive fake fish nets at a craft store.

SCENIC ROUTE → Cut fish shapes out of construction paper and fill the second net with them (along with the heavy objects). Mist kids with spray bottles as they're in the boat, to simulate the spray from the lake.

the net in the water, pulling it back, throwing it in again. They fished and fished and fished, but never caught a single fish. It was a tough night; they already felt so down and sad, and now they couldn't even catch any fish!

Ask: • **How do you think they must have felt at this point?**

• **When have you felt really down and then something else bad happened on top of that?**

As the sun started to come up, they saw someone standing off in the distance on the shore. Either turn on a light or use a flashlight to simulate the rising sun. Shade your eyes and look toward the fire you created, as if you can see someone standing on the shore near the fire.

Say: **Who was it standing there? They all craned their necks and squinted their eyes to try to see who it was. Then the person spoke to them, "Friends, have you caught any fish?"** Have kids shout "No!" as if they're yelling to a person on the beach.

Say: **The person spoke to them again, "Throw out your net on the right-hand side of the boat, and you'll get plenty of fish!" What a strange thing for a person to say. But the disciples figured they could try it out.** Encourage kids to go to the other side of the boat and lift up the heavy net.

Say: **Oh, my goodness, this net is so heavy! There must be a thousand fish in this net!** Drag the net onto the boat, and pretend it's filled with fish. **Wow, how did that man on the beach know we'd catch so many fish on this side of the boat?**

Then one of the disciples suddenly realized who the man on the shore was—it was Jesus! They turned the boat to go to shore and see Jesus. Encourage kids to pretend they're rowing the boat back to shore; then climb out of the boat and go sit around the fire.

Say: **Jesus had made a fire for the disciples and was cooking fish and bread for them. "Bring some of the fish you've just caught," he told them. Then they all sat around the fire together and ate the fish and bread.** Hand out the fish-shaped crackers and snack together quietly for a little bit.

Say: **Imagine how the disciples must have felt right about now. They're so tired and sad and worn out, but here's Jesus offering them food and his friendship again.**

Ask: • **When has someone you loved made you feel better when you were sad?**

SCENIC ROUTE → Bring in sardines or tuna and crackers for kids to try while they sit around the fire. Tell kids this is similar to what the disciples would have been eating with Jesus—and this was for breakfast. Allergy Alert: Check with parents about allergies and dietary concerns.

• **Why did Jesus want to feed and encourage the disciples?**

Say: **After breakfast Jesus talked to his friend Peter. Peter felt terrible about Jesus' death, and even more than that, Peter felt very, very guilty for denying Jesus before his death. But Jesus wasn't mad at Peter. Jesus wanted to forgive Peter and restore him. Jesus told Peter to follow him and to feed his sheep.**

Ask: • **Why do you think Jesus said what he did to Peter?**

• **When did someone forgive you? How did that make you feel?**

• **How would Peter's second chance restore him and renew his strength?**

Say: **The disciples were worn down and tired. Jesus came to them during their darkest point, and he encouraged them and restored their strength. His love and his encouragement renewed them. His encouragement, love, and forgiveness gave them strength to go on and to do the work that Jesus asked them to do. God's power made them strong. In the same way, God encourages us and gives us the strength we need to continue on, even in the hardest of times.**
🌀 **God's power makes us strong.**

(15 minutes)
Life's Misses
Kids will think about how to turn to God when life's "misses" come along.

Say: **We're going to play a game right now that's kind of like basketball.** Have kids form groups of five. Give each group several pingpong balls and a pot. Direct them to place the pot on the ground and then stand about five to 10 feet away from the pot. Challenge them to try to toss the pingpong balls into the pot. Give them three to five minutes to play. They can throw the balls as many times as possible, keeping track of how many times they throw and how many times they miss. Throw in some challenges—turn on a fan, or walk through and knock some balls out of the air. After time's up, ask kids to report their scores. Add them all up and write down on a whiteboard or a large piece of paper how many total shots were made and how many were missed.

Ask: • **What kinds of things happen in life that make you feel just like you did when your ball landed in the pot?**

• **What kinds of things make you feel like you did when your ball missed the pot?**

FUN FACT The Sea of Galilee is the lowest freshwater lake on earth and sits at 700 feet below sea level. Jesus spent much of his ministry time near the Sea of Galilee; he told half his parables there and performed most of his miracles by its waters. During the 1st century, the three types of fish were most commonly referred to were sardines, musht fish, and catfish. It's likely most of the fish caught that night were musht fish, commonly called "St Peter's fish."

Items to Pack: Bibles, pingpong balls (available in bulk at discount stores), a pot or bowl for every five children, whiteboard and dry erase marker, or pen and paper

TOUR GUIDE TIP Form groups of mixed ages for this experience. But allow younger kids to stand closer to the pot and challenge older kids to try getting farther and farther away from the pot as they play.

Say: **Unfortunately, no matter how good we are or how nice we are, or how hard we try, our lives will never be perfect. Just like no matter how good at throwing that ball you were, you still couldn't get it into the pot every time. And sometimes outside forces knocked your ball out—something you had no control over.**

Satan, our enemy, has a lot of power over this earth, and he causes pain and suffering in order to pull us away from God. In heaven, there'll no longer be any pain or hurt, but until we live in heaven with God, we'll encounter pain and hardship. However, God doesn't leave us alone to suffer all by ourselves. He's with us and gives us strength and encouragement for the tough times. ◗God's power makes us strong.

Let's look at a few more verses that show how God can give us strength during hard times.

Give each group one of the passages below. If you have more than three groups, assign the passages to more than one group as needed.

Group 1: Jeremiah 33:10-11

Group 2: Romans 5:3-5

Group 3: Genesis 21:14-19

Write the following questions on the board or on a large piece of paper so each group can see them as they work.

Say: **Read these verses out loud in your group, and then answer these questions.**

Ask: **• How were the people in these verses suffering?**

• How did God promise to restore them or use their suffering for good?

• How can these verses help you trust in God's power to make you strong when you're suffering or in pain?

Walk around the room while children work, and help them as needed. After several minutes, gather kids and talk about what they learned. Give each group a few minutes to share what they discovered.

Afterward say: **Life can be hard—whether we did anything to deserve it or not—but God gives us hope. He renews our strength when we're tired and worn down. He promises us eternal life, when we'll no longer suffer or feel pain. And he promises to be with us always— even in the darkest of times. Because of these promises, we have hope. We can know that ◗God's power makes us strong.**

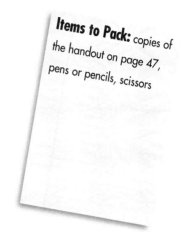

Items to Pack: copies of the handout on page 47, pens or pencils, scissors

SOUVENIRS (10 minutes)

Full to Overflowing

This craft is a reminder that God will renew us and make us strong.

Say: **God wants us to remember to come to him when we're hurting or in pain. We might be tempted to seek other things to make us feel better: playing video games, eating ice cream, or buying a new toy. While those things might make us feel better for a little bit, only God can truly renew us and restore our strength.**

Give kids each a copy of the handout.

Say: **Let's create a souvenir that will help us remember that only God can renew us and only God's power makes us strong.**

Say: **The disciples tried to go fishing to make themselves feel better, but the truth was, only Jesus could really encourage them. Then the first thing he did to encourage them was to help them catch a lot of fish!**

Have kids cut out the fish net with the tab on top of it from the handout. Be sure they don't cut off the tab—they'll need it to make the craft work.

Say: **Now turn over the net and write the answer to this question. You won't have to show your answer to anyone else.**

Ask: • **What's a problem you're facing in your life where you need God to give you strength?**

Next have kids cut the dotted line under the boat. Then tell kids to each place the net underneath their paper, but pull the tab up through the dotted line. Then show kids how they can continue pulling the tab up through the dotted line so it will bring the net of fish up out of the water.

Say: **Each time you pull the net up out of the water, let it remind you that God will give you strength to deal with the problem you wrote on the back of the net. Nothing is too heavy for God. Jesus knew just what the disciples needed to restore their hope and renew their strength; he can do the same for you. God's power makes us strong.**

Have kids place their handouts in their Travel Journals.

**HOME
AGAIN
PRAYER**

(up to 5 minutes)

Have kids form a circle. Tell them to crouch low with their hands on the floor.

Say: **Remember at the beginning of our time today, we got very low to the ground when we talked about events that would make us feel sad? Well, now we're going to demonstrate how God can renew us and give us strength. As we pray, stand up taller and taller and taller. Then when I say "amen," jump up as high as you can!**

Pray: **God, we know that sometimes we'll face hard times in this life. We'll be sad and hurt. But we also know that you love us and we can turn to you when we're in pain. Thank you for renewing us and for giving us strength through your power. In Jesus' name. Amen.**

**FUN
FACT**

The average NBA player can only jump 28 inches into the air from a standing position. Shaquille O'Neal could jump 32 inches. Michael Jordan hit 48 inches, and Kadour Ziani made a world record with a 60-inch vertical leap.

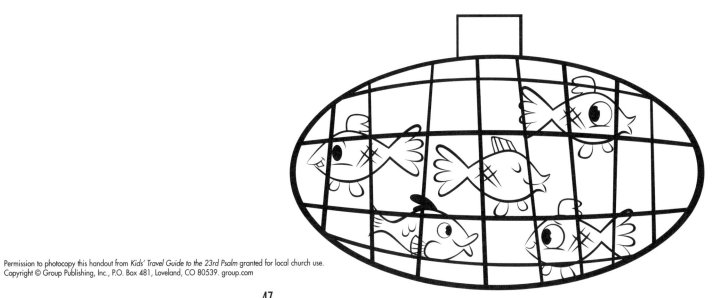

Along Right Paths

JOURNEY 6

Pathway Point: God shows us the way we should go.

In-Focus Verse: "He guides me along right paths, bringing honor to his name" (Psalm 23:3b).

Travel Itinerary

"No, don't do that!" Children learn those words early on as parents try to guide and protect them. But what's true obedience? While following rules might be the beginning of obedience, God wants his children to do the right thing because that's what we want to do...because our hearts are becoming more and more a reflection of God's own heart. Help children see that God is after more than rule-following, and help them understand that God will guide them to make right decisions—that he's placed the Holy Spirit in their hearts to help them become more and more like him.

TOUR GUIDE TIP

The experiences in this book have been designed for multi-age groups. Select from the experiences, or adapt them as needed.

DEPARTURE PRAYER (up to 5 minutes)

Have kids stand in a line, one behind the other, with you at the front.

Say: **Have you ever thought about how trains absolutely have to follow their tracks? They can't just go off driving through a field, or take a turn to the right or left if they feel like it. Nope, they have to stay on their tracks or they can't go anywhere. We're going to be a train right now, so grab onto the waist of the person in front of you. You have to follow that person, no matter which way they go. When I call out, "Switch tracks," whoever I name will break off and start a new train and head in a new direction.**

Lead the train of kids around the room, taking fun turns around a few obstacles. Then call, "Switch tracks, [child's name]" and have that child lead the line behind him or her as a new train. Keep breaking into smaller units until every train is only two or three kids in length.

Ask: • **What happened to our train after we started switching tracks?**

• **Why do trains operate on tracks, instead of being free to go anywhere—like a car, for example? What's the benefit of the tracks?**

48

Say: **Following the tracks is kind of like following God's voice. When we listen to God's voice and follow his ways, he'll guide us in the right direction. Unlike trains, though, we're free to choose. We don't have to stay on the tracks. But when we get off the tracks— when we don't listen to God's voice and we disobey him—we'll end up getting stuck, just as trains do.**

Ask: • **What's your least favorite rule you have to obey at school? at home?**

• **Tell about a time you chose to disobey a rule and what happened.**

Say: **Let's ask God to help us be obedient and follow his path.**

Pray: **Dear God, thank you for guiding us along the right paths and for**  **showing us the way we should go. Help us to always listen to your voice and follow your ways. In Jesus' name. Amen.**

STOP — (10 minutes)
I Can't Hear You!

Children will try to discern the voices of their partners among a cacophony of other noises.

Have kids stand up and face you.

Say: **God watches over us and cares for us, and he gives us peace and renews our strength. God also guides us along right paths.** **God shows us the way we should go. The 23rd Psalm says, "[The Lord] guides me along right paths, bringing honor to his name." God gives us wisdom and helps us know the right thing to do, but we have to learn how to hear God's voice—especially among all the other voices and noises we hear.**

Ask: • **What does it sound like when God talks to you?**

• **What other noises can drown out God's voice so we don't hear him?**

Say: **God's voice can sometimes seem very quiet compared to all the other loud noises in our lives: the noises of television, the Internet, our friends, the music we listen to. These aren't bad things, but they can be really loud, and it can be easier to listen to them than to God. In the Bible, John 10:2-5 tells us that we can recognize God's voice. It says, "For the one who enters through the gate is the shepherd of the sheep. The gatekeeper opens the gate for him, and the sheep recognize his voice and come to him."**

FUN FACT The Swansea and Mumbles railway service is officially recognized as the world's first passenger train. In 1807, a railroad carriage was converted to carry people. Still drawn by horse—but traveling along rails—the carriage traveled along the perimeter of Swansea Bay in Wales.

Items to Pack: blindfolds, energetic worship CD, CD player

Let's play a game now to see if we can recognize a familiar voice among a lot of other noises.

Form pairs, and have one partner blindfold the other. Then have those who aren't blindfolded pick spots about 10 feet away from their partners and stay there. Explain that each blindfolded person will listen closely for his or her partner's voice and try to find that person. Partners can use clues such as "I'm over here—walk right! You're getting warmer." Then turn on the music loud so kids will have to shout to try to lead their partners to them. When pairs find each other, have them reverse roles and play again.

After partners have had a chance to play both roles, have kids come back together and sit in a circle.

Ask: • **What made it easy or difficult to hear your partner's voice?**

• **How were you able to find and concentrate on your partner's voice?**

• **How's this like trying to find God's voice in all the other noises and voices in our lives?**

• **What helps you stay focused on listening for God's voice?**

Say: **There's often so much going on in our lives that it's hard to pick out God's voice and listen to it. But we can learn to recognize his voice and follow it. ●God shows us the way we should go, and when we follow him, God will guide us to lead lives that honor him.**

STORY EXCURSION

(15 minutes)
Follow the Clues

Children will uncover the details of a mysterious death as they learn the importance of following God's path.

Photocopy the clues from page 55, and cut them apart. You'll hang on to the first clue and hide the others. Create four signs: King's Bedroom, Daniel's Room, Public Square, and Banquet Hall. Then place the signs and clues as follows. *King's Bedroom:* Hide Clue #2 under a journal and place it in one corner of your room, along with a few other journal-type books. *Daniel's House:* Hide Clue #3 under a notebook on a desk. *Public Square:* Crumple Clue #4 and place it somewhere on the floor near the Banquet Hall. *Banquet Hall:* Hide Clue #5 in a plastic goblet or cup in another corner of the room. You'll also need to write the words *Mene, Mene, Tekel, Parsin* on a large piece of newsprint and tape it to a wall in the banquet hall.

Have kids stand near you. Act as if you've just gotten some big news.

Say: **Everyone, everyone come here! This just in—I've just heard that evil King Belshazzar of Babylon has been killed.** Hold up Clue #1. **Here's the decree from our new king, "I am Darius the Mede, the new king of Babylon. I have vanquished King Belshazzar and taken the throne."**

I need your help to find clues and unravel this mystery. Look carefully and see what you can find at King Belshazzar's, Daniel's, and the banquet hall. When you find clues, bring them back here to me. Give kids time to search the room and discover all the clues.

When they've found everything, say: **It looks like you've found a lot of clues. Let's read them in order and see if we can figure out what happened.**

Look at Clue #2 and say: **This is written by King Belshazzar himself; it says, "I'm going to die tonight. Daniel knew. He told me." King Belshazzar knew he was going to die!**

Ask: • **How could he have known? What do you think?** Let kids respond and talk about it together.

Say: **We should find out how Daniel knew. Maybe the next clue will help us discover how all this happened.**

Hold up Clue #3 and read it aloud for everyone to hear: **"There was strange writing on the wall. I knew it was from God. It read 'Mene, Mene, Tekel, Parsin.' I translated it to mean that God had numbered King Belshazzar's days as king, and they were now over. Belshazzar failed God and his kingdom would now be divided."**

Say: **Oh, wow. This is an unexpected clue.**

Ask: • **What do you think it means? What does it mean that there was writing on the wall? Who wrote on the wall? Why would God send a note on a wall?** Give kids time to respond to your questions as you try to figure out the mystery together.

Hold up Clue #4 and smooth it out.

Say: **Look at this crumpled up paper. It says, "By royal decree, all the wise men, magicians, enchanters, astrologers, and fortune tellers should report to the king to translate the writing on the wall!"**

Belshazzar must've summoned Daniel to read the writing, too, and God must've given Daniel the wisdom to understand the writing. That's why Daniel knew ahead of time that the king would die.

Ask: • **But why would God want the king to die?** Pause for kids to comment.

TOUR GUIDE TIP

Events in the Bible are certainly not all PG-rated. In this story, a king dies—is murdered, in fact. While gory details are kept out of this lesson, you'll want to pay attention to your youngest children and make sure they aren't scared or uncomfortable.

SCENIC ROUTE →

Make everyone feel like a detective! Bring in magnifying glasses, fedoras, and fake mustaches for each child. Play background music from a spy or detective movie.

Say: **This last clue looks like a note written to the king's servants. What does it say?** Have one of the children read the note: "Bring out the gold and silver cups that were stolen from the Temple of God. The king wants to use them for his party—to toast his idols made of gold, silver, bronze, iron, wood, and stone."

Say: **King Belshazzar used the sacred goblets from the Temple of God in order to worship fake gods! What a terrible thing to do. Listen as I read what Daniel said to King Belshazzar.**

Then read aloud Daniel 5:23-28, 30-31.

Ask: • **Why was what King Belshazzar did so wrong?**

• **Why do you think Daniel was able to hear God's voice and understand what God had written on the walls when no one else could?**

• **How was God able to use Daniel because Daniel listened to God's voice and followed him?**

• **How might God use you if you listen to his voice as Daniel did?**

Say: **It isn't always easy to hear God's voice or to do what he wants, but it's the best way to live. When we follow God's path, our lives are better—we can experience the life that God wants us to have. That doesn't mean that everything will always be perfect and happy—we talked about that last week—but it does mean that we'll always honor God by listening for him to show us the way we should go.**

(10 minutes)
Choose Your Own Adventure

ADVENTURES IN GROWING

Kids will realize that God has provided ways for us to hear his voice—through Scripture, teachers, and the Holy Spirit.

Say: **We've been talking about how important it is to listen to God's voice because he'll show us the way we should go. But how do we hear God's voice when God doesn't write on the wall or talk out loud to us? Let's see what the Bible has to say about this.**

Have kids form three groups, and assign each group one of the following Scripture passages:

Group 1: John 14:15-17

Group 2: 2 Timothy 3:16-17

Group 3: Hebrews 13:16-17

Have kids in each group answer these questions:

• **What does your Scripture passage tell us about how to hear God's voice?**

Items to Pack: Bibles, basket, 3x5 cards, pens

• **What's an example of how God speaks to you in this way?**

• **What would help you hear God's voice better when he speaks to you like this?**

Then have a child from each small group share what the group learned. Afterward give children each a 3x5 card and a pen, and have them describe a situation where they need God's help to decide what to do. Tell kids not to write any names or anything that would identify them because others will read the cards. For example, someone might write, "My mom wants me to keep playing soccer, but I want to only play tennis and get better at that."

After all the kids have finished writing, pick up the cards, put them in a basket, and shuffle them around. Have kids take turns drawing out one card at a time, reading it aloud, and then giving an example of how they'd seek God's wisdom for that situation. For example, a child might say, "I'd pray about it and then talk to an adult to get advice."

Say: **In every situation, we can seek God's will and ask him to help us make the right choice. It may not be easy to hear him, but God has given us ways to recognize his voice and follow him.**  **God will show us the way we should go.**

SOUVENIRS (10 minutes)
Listen 'Up'!

This craft is a reminder that we need to listen to God so he can show us the way to go.

Make a copy of the handout on page 56, and fold one for each child.

Say: **God wants us to listen to his voice and follow his path in all situations. But, as we know, sometimes it's very hard to hear God's quiet voice in the midst of all the other people and things trying to get our attention.**

Give kids a copy of the handout.

Say: **On one side of this handout, there are a lot of "voices" talking into this person's ear. I want you to take a minute to write all the different voices that talk into your ear. For example, by the person you might write the names of some friends at school who often try to tell you what to think or what to do—sometimes it's okay advice, but other times you know it's wrong. Or next to the TV, you might write a couple of your favorite shows and how they influence what you think. Identify at least one thing in your life for each of the pictures.**

If you have some kids who are too young to write out their tough situations, have an older child help them.

Items to Pack: copies of the handout on page 56, crayons, colored pencils

Give kids several minutes to write. Tell younger kids to draw pictures, or help them write on their papers.

Say: **Now turn the handout over. God is talking to you, too. He's trying to get your attention and show you the right path to travel.** 🌑 **God shows us the way we should go. Write one way you're going to listen to God's voice this week.**

Give kids a few minutes to write. Then say: **Now get with a partner and talk about what you wrote on both sides of your paper. Answer these questions with your partner.**

Ask: • **What other voices keep you from hearing God's voice?**

• **What can you do this week to recognize God's voice better?**

Say: **God loves us and wants the best for our lives. He is there talking to us and pointing us down the right path. We just need to be aware of his voice and willing to listen to him. When we do,** 🌑**God will show us the way we should go.**

HOME AGAIN PRAYER

(up to 5 minutes)

Have kids stay with their partners for this prayer.

Say: **Each of you will pray for your partner. Pray, specifically, that your partner would be able to hear God's voice this week by doing whatever your partner wrote on the back of the handout. Pray that your partner would hear God's voice over all the other noises on the front side. I'll give you a few minutes to pray; then I'll close.** Wait several minutes until kids have finished praying for each other.

Then pray: **God, we know that you love us and want the best for our lives. We pray that we can learn to recognize your voice and follow you. Thank you for** 🌑**showing us the way we should go. In Jesus' name. Amen.**

Have kids place their finished handouts in their Travel Journals.

FUN FACT According to a 2009 study done for Consumer Kids, children now spend, on average, about twice as much time annually in front of a TV or computer screen than they do in the classroom—2,000 hours in front of a screen, compared with 900 in the classroom and only 1,270 hours with their parents.

Clue#1

*I am Darius the Mede,
the new king of Babylon.
I have vanquished King Belshazzar
and taken the throne.*

Clue#2

I'M GOING TO DIE TONIGHT.

DANIEL KNEW.

HE TOLD ME.

Clue#3

There was strange writing on the wall. I knew it was from God, it read "Mene, Mene, Tekel, Parsin." I translated it to mean that God had numbered King Belshazzar's days as king, and they were now over. Belshazzar failed God and his kingdom would now be divided.

Clue#4

By royal decree, all the wise men, magicians, enchanters, astrologers and fortunetellers should report to the king to translate the writing on the wall.

Clue#5

Bring out the gold and silver cups that had been stolen from the Temple of God. The King wants to use them for his party—to toast his idols made of gold, silver, bronze, iron, wood, and stone.

Through the Darkest Valley

Pathway Point: God helps us overcome our fears.

In-Focus Verse: "Even when I walk through the darkest valley, I will not be afraid, for you are close beside me" (Psalm 23:4a).

Travel Itinerary

To lose one's family is the greatest fear for most people—whether children or adults. But for women like Naomi in biblical times, this catastrophic loss carried with it an additional disaster: poverty. Without other people's kindness, Naomi would've died because there was no means for her to survive on her own. Though God placed provisions for widows and orphans into his law, these weren't always followed—Boaz was an exception. You can imagine Naomi's fear and pain. She surely would have been walking through the darkest of valleys... and yet God was with her. He comforted and provided for Naomi through her daughter-in-law Ruth and through Boaz. God didn't abandon Naomi in her darkest valley, and he won't abandon us. Teach your children that God loves us and will be with us in the darkest of times—when we're afraid and alone. He'll help us overcome our fears.

> **TOUR GUIDE TIP** The experiences in this book have been designed for multi-age groups. Select from the experiences, or adapt them as needed.

DEPARTURE PRAYER (up to 5 minutes)

Have kids gather in a circle around you.

Say: **Think about a time you felt scared and lonely. Most of us have felt very scared and very lonely at some point in our lives. Maybe when we're by ourselves in a new place, or when we go to bed and all the lights are off. Find a lonely spot in the room, apart from everyone else.**

> **SCENIC ROUTE →** Shut off all the lights during the opening prayer so kids feel even more alone.

Give kids a minute or so to find a spot.

Say: **Now close your eyes and put your arms out.** (Pause.) **Can you feel anyone? Nope. There's no one anywhere close to you.** (Pause.) **Now keep your eyes closed and remember the loneliest you've ever felt. Think of what that was like.** (Pause.)

Even though you felt like you were all by yourself and no one was there to help you, God was with you. Now put your arms around yourself, and give yourself a hug. (Pause.) **God is always with you!**

Open your eyes now, and let's thank God for being with us always and for helping us overcome the fears that come with loneliness.

Pray: **Dear God, we know that even when we're all by ourselves and there isn't another person anywhere close to us, you're with us. Thank you for helping us not be afraid. In Jesus' name. Amen.**

Think you've ever felt lonely? Imagine being hundreds of miles above the earth's surface, suspended in space, looking back at earth. That's lonely. But this is what astronauts aboard the space station go through every day. Astronaut Shannon Lucid, who spent 188 days on the Mir space station, described life aboard the space station like this: "I think going to work on a daily basis on Mir is very similar to going to work on a daily basis on an out-station in Antarctica. The big difference with going to work here is the isolation—because you really are isolated. You don't have a lot of support from the ground. You really are on your own."

1st STOP DISCOVERY (10 minutes)
Monsters Under the Bed!

Children will work together to draw a picture that represents their fears.

Say: **God watches over us and cares for us. He gives us peace, renews our strength, and guides us along right paths. God also helps us when we're scared.** 🌓**God helps us overcome our fears. The 23rd Psalm says, "Even when I walk through the darkest valley, I will not be afraid, for you are close beside me."**

Ask: • **What do you picture when you hear the words** *dark valley?*
• **When have you felt very lonely or very scared?**
• **What helped you feel better?**

Say: **Sometimes we imagine monsters under our beds or in our closets. Of course, there aren't really monsters in our closets! But monsters often represent a lot of other fears that we have: fears of the dark, fears of being left alone, or fears of getting hurt. We're going to get into small groups and create our own very scary monsters.** Form groups of three to five, depending on the number of children. Give each group a large sheet of newsprint, several markers, glue, and craft supplies.

Say: **Okay, now in your group, work together to create the scariest monster you can think of. Draw an outline first, and then fill it in using the markers; then use the glue and craft supplies to give it more of a 3-D appearance. Everyone work together to imagine the scariest monster possible.** Give kids several minutes to do this. Walk around to the different groups and help them out as needed. After kids are finished, have them come back together as a group to listen to your next set of instructions.

Say: **Think of the scariest thing you can imagine. Maybe it's being lost in the middle of a big store or a big city, or maybe it's being out in the woods at night, or maybe it's being in a fierce storm. Whatever it is, go back to your drawing and write that thing next to the monster.** Give kids about a minute to get back in their groups and each write their

Items to Pack: large sheets of newsprint; markers; glue; various craft supplies: string, buttons, chenille wires, ribbon

individual fears next to their group's monster. Encourage older kids to help younger kids write if needed. Once all the kids are finished writing, have them come back together and show off their pictures to the other groups. Give the kids in each group a minute or so to explain their monster and read off their fears to the other kids.

Say: **Even though our monsters aren't real, they do look scary! And they represent these very real fears we've written down.**

Ask: **• Why are these fears we've written down so scary?**

• How do you think God can help us with our fears?

Say: **Scary things are probably going to happen to every one of us in our lives. We can't avoid getting scared, but we can turn to God when we're scared. God can help us do the right thing in that scary situation, and God can help us feel less scared and more at peace.**  **God helps us overcome our fears. Right now, let's listen to a story about a woman who really did have to face the scariest thing she could've ever imagined happening to her. But**  **God helped her overcome her fears.**

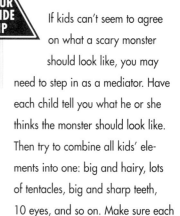

If kids can't seem to agree on what a scary monster should look like, you may need to step in as a mediator. Have each child tell you what he or she thinks the monster should look like. Then try to combine all kids' elements into one: big and hairy, lots of tentacles, big and sharp teeth, 10 eyes, and so on. Make sure each child has at least one element represented in the final picture.

STORY EXCURSION

(15 minutes)
The Scariest of All Things

Children will hear about the trials of two women and learn that God will help them overcome their fears, even in the scariest situations.

Items to Pack: Bible, story script on pages 64-66, poster board for signs, marker

Make three signs ahead of time. The first should have "HAPPY" written on it, the second "SAD," and the third "SCARED." Make sure the letters are big enough for kids to read from a bit of a distance. You'll also need to make seven copies of the script.

Gather kids together in a large group.

Say: **The Bible tells us about a woman named Naomi—if Naomi had written her biggest fear next to our monster today, she would've written exactly what happened to her. Naomi had to face her biggest fear, and she discovered she could trust God to help her overcome it. Let's find out what happened.**

Kids will act out the story. Assign the roles and then hand out copies of the script to the actors.

SCENIC ROUTE → Bring in pre-ground barley to show kids what the barley Ruth picked would've look like before she ground it into flour to make bread. Use a mortar and pestle to grind up some of the barley so kids can see how much work it would've been.

You'll need the following roles filled:

Narrator

Sign Person

Naomi

Ruth

Orpah

Woman of Bethlehem

Boaz

Tell the rest of the kids that they have an important part to play as well—following along and reacting to the Sign Person's directions.

Say: **When the Sign Person holds up the HAPPY sign, act and sound happy. Show me what it's like for you to get happy.** Give kids a few seconds to demonstrate how they'll convey being happy. **When the Sign Person holds up the SAD sign, act and sound sad. Show me what it's like for you to be sad.** Give kids a few seconds to demonstrate how they'll show sadness. **When the Sign Person holds up the SCARED sign, act really scared. Show me what this looks and sounds like.** Give kids a few seconds to demonstrate. **Okay, let's start our play!**

Tell actors to follow along with the script and act out or read their parts.

After the play is over, have kids applaud everyone's participation. Then have kids sit in a circle.

Ask: • **Why is it hard to trust God during really hard times when you're sad or scared?**

• **Where did you see God in Ruth and Naomi's story?**

• **What can you do that would help you remember to trust God during really hard times when you're sad or scared?**

Say: **The things that happen in this world aren't always good. Bad things happen to good people sometimes. But the truth is, God is always with us. He loves us and will help us even in the darkest times. God was with Naomi, and God gave Naomi a companion and friend in Ruth. God didn't abandon Naomi, but cared for her and provided for her. God helped her overcome her fear, her pain, and her very hard situation. 🕐God will also help us overcome our fears.**

FUN FACT

Ruth gathered an "ephah" of barley from Boaz' fields in one day. That's about 30 pounds of barley. She would have made up to 60 small loaves of bread with that much barley!

ADVENTURES IN GROWING

(10 minutes)
Strangers in a Strange Land

Kids will feel uncomfortable as they try to make their way in a strange land.

Items to Pack: snack, paper, markers, foreign language dictionary or go to dictionary.com

Hide a snack somewhere in your room ahead of time—make sure it's in a tough-to-find spot that kids would never see on their own. Then write a series of clues to help kids find the snack. For example, the first clue could say, "Go to the blue book shelf to find the next clue." Then that clue would direct them to the third clue, and so on, until the last clue leads them to the snack. Write at least five clues. Then use a foreign language dictionary to create new clue signs that say the same thing, but in the foreign language. Place the foreign language clues in the appropriate spots in the room. Save the English clues for later.

Say: **I have a scavenger hunt all set up for you, and if you follow the clues, you'll find a treat. The clues are taped around the room.** Point to the first one. **You can start with that one, and then find your way to the next one. Good luck!**

Let kids walk around and try to figure out the clues. Of course, they won't be able to read them...but go ahead and let them try for several minutes. Shrug or speak to them in a foreign language if they ask you questions. After a while, gather kids.

TOUR GUIDE TIP

Allergy Alert: Be sure to check with parents about allergies and dietary concerns before choosing a snack.

Ask: • **Why couldn't you find your snack?**

• **What was it like not being able to read the directions?**

Say: **This may've been how Naomi felt when she first moved to Moab and how Ruth felt when she moved to Bethlehem. It's scary and frustrating to be a stranger in a strange land. You feel uncomfortable, alienated, scared, and even silly—because you can't understand anything!**

Ask: • **When have you felt uncomfortable and scared because you were in a strange place and didn't know exactly what to do—like being at a new school or a party?**

• **How did you adapt and get used to it? Who helped you?**

• **How can you trust God to help you and be with you the next time you have to be in a strange place?**

Hang up the English signs now, and let kids follow those clues to find their snack.

SCENIC ROUTE →

Play a foreign language CD as kids try to navigate their way around. It will add to the authenticity of the activity.

Say: **Being a stranger in a strange place can make us feel more alone and scared than ever. But just as God was with Naomi, God will**

SCENIC ROUTE →

Serve snacks from the origin country of the language you're using. Rice crackers from Japan, plantain chips from Puerto Rico...be creative! Allergy Alert: Be sure to check with parents about allergies and dietary concerns.

Items to Pack: copies of the handout on page 67, black construction paper, white chalk, scissors, glue sticks, whiteboard and marker

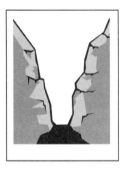

be with you any time you're alone or in an unfamiliar place. 🌀 **God helps us overcome our fears.**

SOUVENIRS → (10 minutes)
God Is With Us

This craft is a reminder that God is with us in the very darkest of places.

Say: **The 23rd Psalm says, "Even when I walk through the darkest valley, I will not be afraid, for you are close beside me." Let's create a souvenir that will help us remember that God is walking with us through the scariest and darkest times in our lives.**

Give each child a copy of the handout, a sheet of black construction paper, a glue stick, and a piece of white chalk.

Say: **On this handout, there are mountains on either side. Cut out the white space between the two mountains. Then glue the handout to the black construction paper.** Give kids several minutes to do this. Assist younger children as needed.

Now on the black paper, draw a picture of a person walking between the mountains, and then add part of our verse for today: "I will not be afraid, for you are close beside me." Write the verse on a whiteboard or newsprint for everyone to see, and give kids a few minutes. **Now somewhere else on your page, write one thing you're scared about—it could be something you know you're going to have to do soon, such as going to summer camp, starting a new sport, or moving to a new school. Or it could be a situation or worry that makes you fearful. Write it on your paper.** Pause for a few minutes.

Now get together with a partner and talk about what you wrote on your paper. Answer these questions together:

Ask: • **Why are you afraid about what you wrote on your paper?**

• **How can you trust God to help you overcome your fear?**

Say: **When we face something new or strange, it's easy to get scared. But God wants us to know that we're not alone and that he never abandons us. We can pray to him for strength, for peace, for joy—and 🌀 God will help us overcome our fears.**

HOME AGAIN PRAYER

(up to 5 minutes)

Have kids bring their Souvenirs to prayer time.

Say: **Look at your handout while we pray today. In the middle of the prayer, I'm going to pause so you can pray silently. During that pause, pray about the situation you wrote on your paper. Pray that God would help you over-**come your fear.

Pray: **God, thank you so much for Ruth and Naomi. You showed us through them that you never abandon us or leave us alone—even when we're scared and alone, you're there for us, and you help us overcome. I pray for everyone in this room. Remind all of us that we can turn to you in our scariest times, and you'll be with us and help us. We pray now that you'll help us overcome our fears about the situations we've written on our handouts.** Pause for about a minute to let kids pray silently. **God, thank you so much for helping us overcome our fears. In Jesus' name. Amen.**

Have kids place their finished handouts in their Travel Journals.

STORY SCRIPT

Narrator: This is a true thing that happened in the Bible to a woman named Naomi. She was SAD.

Sign Person: *(Holds up the SAD sign.)*

Naomi: *(Enters from stage left.)*

Narrator: Naomi had lived in Moab for 10 years with her family. But now she was a widow, with no husband and no sons. She had no house, no money, no animals, no anything. She was *very* SAD!

Sign Person: *(Holds up the SAD sign.)*

Narrator: So she decided she'd move back to Bethlehem where she'd been born—but she didn't know if anyone would remember her or help her when she got back. Naomi was SCARED!

Sign Person: *(Holds up the SCARED sign.)*

Narrator: Naomi walked to Bethlehem.

Naomi: *(Starts to walk toward stage right.)*

Ruth and Orpah: *(Enter from stage left and follow Naomi.)*

Narrator: Ruth and Orpah, who'd been married to Naomi's sons, were following Naomi, but she urged them to return to their own homes.

Naomi: Go back to your mothers' homes. And may the Lord reward you for your kindness to your husbands and to me. May the Lord bless you with the security of another marriage.

Narrator: Then she kissed them goodbye, and they all wept because they were so SAD.

Sign Person: *(Holds up the SAD sign.)*

Naomi, Ruth, Orpah: *(Hug each other and pretend to cry.)*

Narrator: Orpah did go back.

Orpah: *(Walks back to stage left, waving over her shoulder at Naomi and Ruth; then sits back down in the audience.)*

Narrator: But Ruth chose to stay with Naomi.

Ruth: Don't ask me to leave you and turn back. Wherever you go, I'll go; wherever you live, I'll live. Your people will be my people, and your God will be my God. Wherever you die, I'll die, and there I'll be buried. May the Lord punish me severely if I allow anything but death to separate us!

Narrator: It made Naomi HAPPY that Ruth chose to stay with her.

Sign Person: *(Holds up the HAPPY sign.)*

Narrator: Naomi was still very SAD, though, because she'd lost everything.

Sign Person: *(Holds up the SAD sign.)*

Narrator: Ruth was also feeling a lot of emotions. She was leaving her home and going to live in a land where she wouldn't know anyone. She wouldn't know the language either, and she wouldn't know what to do. She was SCARED.

Sign Person: *(Holds up the SCARED sign.)*

Ruth and Naomi: *(Exit stage right; then re-enter, moving to center stage.)*

Narrator: When Ruth and Naomi came to Bethlehem the whole town was HAPPY to see them.

Sign Person: *(Holds up the HAPPY sign.)*

Woman of Bethlehem: *(Enters from stage left and greets Naomi with hugs)* Can this be Naomi?

Naomi: Don't call me Naomi. Call me Mara, for it is a bitter lot that the Almighty has sent me. I went away full, and the Lord has brought me back empty.

Narrator: Naomi was still SAD.

Sign Person: *(Holds up the SAD sign.)*

Woman of Bethlehem: *(Exits stage left.)*

Narrator: Now they were back in Bethlehem, but Ruth and Naomi still didn't have any food. They were very SCARED because they didn't know *when* they'd ever have anything to eat.

Sign Person: *[Holds up the SCARED sign.]*

Ruth, Naomi: *[Move to stage left.]*

Narrator: So Ruth decided to go out into the fields and glean barley. This meant that she was allowed to pick up whatever was left on the ground after the owner picked the barley. It wasn't much, but it would keep them from starving.

Ruth: *(Returns to stage center; bends down, pretending to pick up barley and place it in a basket.)*

Narrator: It made Naomi HAPPY that Ruth helped her by gathering the barley.

Sign Person: *(Holds up the HAPPY sign.)*

Narrator: Now Boaz was the owner of the field and saw Ruth gleaning barley from his field.

Boaz: *(Joins Ruth at stage center.)*

Narrator: Boaz was very kind and told his workers to leave even more barley on the ground for Ruth. This made Naomi and Ruth HAPPY!

Sign Person: *(Holds up the HAPPY sign.)*

Narrator: After some time, Boaz made a decision to marry Ruth. He wanted to care for her and for Naomi.

Boaz: *(Gets on one knee in front of Ruth and pretends to propose to her.)*

Narrator: A wedding! This was very exciting! It meant that Ruth and Naomi would be cared for and they wouldn't have to worry about being hungry or alone. Everyone was so HAPPY!

Sign Person: *(Holds up the HAPPY sign.)*

Naomi, Ruth, Boaz: *(Stand in stage center with their arms around each other and act very happy; then all turn briefly with backs to audience; when they turn back to face the audience, Ruth holds her arms as though she's carrying a baby.)*

Narrator: The next year Ruth and Boaz had their first baby, a son they named Obed. Now Naomi was a grandmother, and they were all *very* HAPPY!

Sign Person: *(Holds up the HAPPY sign.)*

Narrator: Later when Obed grew up, he became the father of Jesse. And when Jesse grew up, he became the father of David, the shepherd boy who killed Goliath and became king of Israel—and who was the ancestor of Jesus. For which we are *all* very HAPPY!

Sign Person: *(Holds up the HAPPY sign.)*

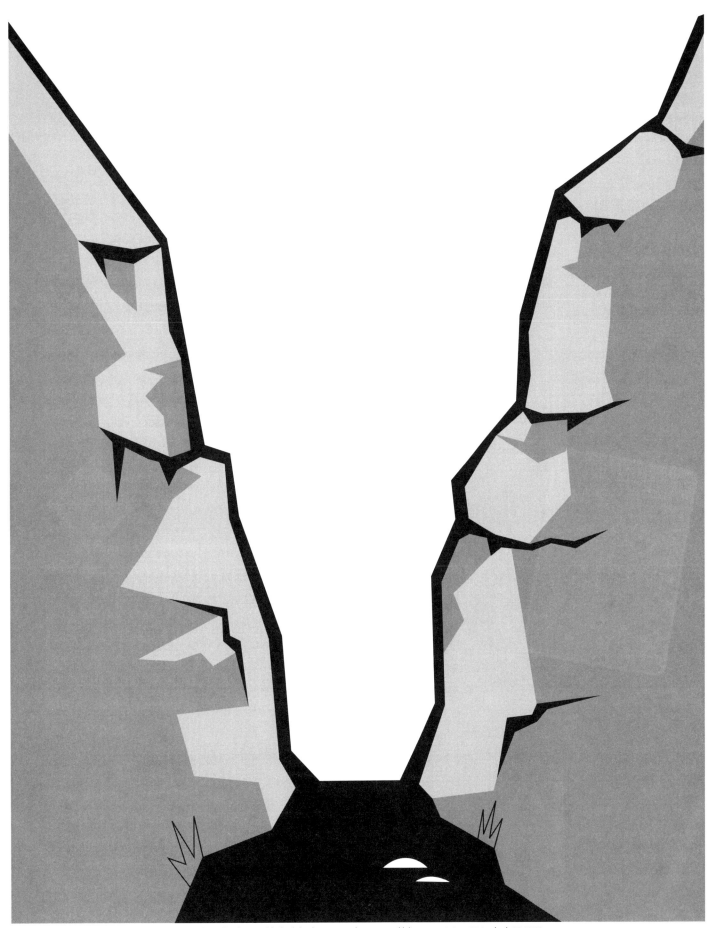

Protection and Comfort

Pathway Point: 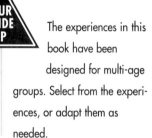 God protects us from harm.

In-Focus Verse: "Your rod and your staff protect and comfort me" (Psalm 23:4c).

Travel Itinerary

This week's verse of the 23rd Psalm helps reassure children that no matter what struggles or challenges we face, God shows his love for us by watching over us and keeping us from harm. We can be certain of God's protection. Kids will learn that the rod and staff symbolize not only our dependence on God for protection and safety but also the deep comfort we draw from his protection. We can trust ⚪ God to protect us from harm.

The experiences in this book have been designed for multi-age groups. Select from the experiences, or adapt them as needed.

DEPARTURE PRAYER (up to 5 minutes)

Have kids sit in a circle and put their hands together in preparation for prayer, palms touching and fingers straight up.

Say: **It may sound funny when the 23rd Psalm describes a rod and a staff as comforting, but a shepherd uses a rod and staff to protect the sheep in a flock. We know that ⚪ God protects us from harm because he's our shepherd and we're part of his flock. Let's bow down our first two fingers on each hand to show that God is in control, not us.** (Pause.) **Keep these two fingers pressed down while keeping your third fingers, the ring fingers, together and pointed toward heaven to remind us of God's rod and staff.** (Show kids how to do this.) **Now without sliding your ring fingers, try to pull them apart as you keep the other fingers pressed together.**

Ask: • **Why do you think you couldn't move your ring fingers away from each other?**

• **How does it feel when you can't do something for yourself?**

• **When have you felt helpless like this?**

• **What helps you during these times?**

Say: **A shepherd has the job of keeping the sheep safe. It's comforting to know that even we when feel helpless, God takes care of us and ⚪ protects us from harm.**

With hands still in the same position, pray: **God, thank you for being our shepherd. We praise you for your power that protects us from harm. Help us look to you for comfort, knowing you're always with us. In Jesus' name. Amen.**

1st STOP DISCOVERY

(10 minutes)
Fort-ified

This game helps kids connect the metaphors of "rod and staff" to the idea of God comforting us.

Items to Pack: Bible, newspapers, tape, cloth napkins or bandannas

Ahead of time, collect double-page sections of newspaper, enough so that you and each child have two. You'll also need enough cloth napkins or bandannas so you and each child will have one.

Hand out two double-pages of newspaper and a cloth napkin to each child.

Say: **Today's verse from the 23rd Psalm says, "Your rod and your staff protect and comfort me." The rods and staffs of a shepherd provide different kinds of protection for the sheep. The shepherd usually carved his rod, which was a heavy, short stick with a knob on the end. Let's each tie a big knot in the cloth napkin to make ourselves a rod.** Give everyone time to do this.

Say: **The rod could be used close-up for defense or thrown as a weapon if something or someone threatened the sheep. Let's throw our rods so they land in different parts of the room.** Have kids throw their rods.

Next have kids each take their two double-page sections of newspaper and follow your actions as you roll up your newspaper sections: Open the first double-page section and lay it flat. Then roll up one page to the fold in the middle, and place the edge of another two-page section against the roll. Continue rolling up the pages in the same direction, and tape the finished roll in the middle so it stays closed.

Then hold up the newspaper roll, and show the children how to slowly pull out the inside of the newspaper roll so it becomes longer. This "staff" can now be folded at the top to make a crook.

Say: **The staff was a longer piece of wood that had a curve at the end. The shepherd used this to draw a sheep to him if it started to wander off or to gently pull a sheep away from a dangerous place like a mountain ledge. The shepherd used the staff to count the sheep, and like the rod, it could also be used as a weapon. Now let's each find a**

TOUR GUIDE TIP Check to see if your church's props include a shepherd's staff, so children can see what one looks like. Otherwise, try to find a wooden walking stick to show today's equivalent of a staff.

FUN FACT A rod was also used as a measuring distance hundreds of years ago. Four rods equaled 66 feet, and there are 66 books in the Bible for us to travel, too!

SCENIC ROUTE →

As an alternative game, lay the rods and staffs in the middle of the room to create a "safe circle." In this version of Red Light, Green Light, have a caller say, "Rod and staff" to get kids to walk closer to the caller and away from the circle. When the caller says, "Comfort me" have all the kids get into the circle as quickly as possible and shout together, "Safe!"

Items to Pack: Bibles, 3x5 cards, pens

place on the floor to leave a staff so we can play a game using the rods and staffs.

After kids have done this, have them gather at the far end of the room; then say: **I'll stand at this end of the room and say, "Rod and staff." Wherever you are, find the closest item, either a rod or staff, and move quickly to pick it up. Every time I say, "Rod and staff," try to move closer to me, but you have to put down whatever you have in your hand and get the nearest opposite object. For example, if you're holding a staff and I say, "Rod and staff," put down the staff, and pick up the nearest rod. When time's up, I'll call out "Comfort me" and move to the center of the room. If you're holding a staff, quickly make a circle around me and hold your staff high up in the air; if you have a rod, make a circle around the people holding the staffs and hold your rod straight out. If I say, "Comfort me" and you aren't holding either a rod or staff, quickly come into the center with me and call "safe." We'll play a few times so others can have a turn being the caller. Let's start.**

Afterward say: **Wherever we go, God protects us from harm. We can take comfort because God is always there for us like an invisible fortress.**

Ask: **• How did this experience help you understand our Bible verse?**

• What's something that makes you feel protected and safe?

• When have you felt like God was protecting you?

Say: **God is our shepherd. Many things happen in our lives that we don't understand, but God is there to comfort and protect us. He wants us to trust him always. We know he's the one in control and he'll take care of us. Let's look at another psalm to learn more about this.**

STORY EXCURSION

(15 minutes)
God's Promise

This psalm re-enactment will remind children about ways that God protects us from harm.

Open your Bible and show children Psalm 121.

Say: **Today we're going to act out Psalm 121, which tells us about some of the many ways God protects us from harm. To help us** remember this psalm, we're going to make up our own sign language for it. Form four groups; give each group a Bible, 3x5 cards, and pens. Assign each group as follows:

Group 1: Psalm 121:1-2

Group 2: Psalm 121:3-4

Group 3: Psalm 121:5-6

Group 4: Psalm 121:7-8

Say: **Work in your groups to come up with simple motions for all of us to do with you. You can make notes on the 3x5 cards if that helps you to remember.**

Give kids time to practice their moves; then have each group say and act out its Bible verses for the rest of the children. Have all the kids mimic the motions of each group as it presents its verse so everyone acts out the passage together.

Ask: • **What can you tell others about how God protects you?**

• **Why is it important to tell others that God is always protecting us?**

Say: **In the psalm we acted out, we learned how actively** 🌑 **God protects us from harm. We learned how he watches over us all the time, wherever we go. We also learned that he never stops protecting us and that he will keep watch over us in the future, too. It's comforting to know he constantly cares for us.**

Ask: • **How does God keep you from stumbling?**

• **In what ways does God act as your "shade" to protect you from harm?**

• **How is a shepherd a good description for God?**

• **What are some other words you can think of to describe how God protects us?**

Say: **God protects us in so many ways. He loves us and cares for us better than any shepherd cares for his sheep. We trust him because he has power over everything and he loves us.**

ADVENTURES IN GROWING

(15 minutes)

God's Comfort Zone

Kids will look at Scripture to discover more about God's promises of comfort and protection.

Gather kids and say: **We've been learning that God shows his love for us by watching over us and keeping us from harm. God doesn't just**

SCENIC ROUTE →

For an alternative, have kids work together on a poster board to change the nouns in Psalm 121 into picture symbols so the psalm can easily be shared with a group of younger children.

TOUR GUIDE TIP

As they work in different groups, if you notice that the chosen "sign language" movements of the groups are too similar to each other, ask groups to add foot movement, crouching, or stretching to their hand motions.

FUN FACT

Another definition of the word *staff* is someone who supports the boss to complete a job, just like the stick does for the shepherd!

Items to Pack: Bibles, large sheets of poster board, markers, craft supplies

want to keep us from harm, though; God wants his love to make us feel comfortable and safe. Let's think about what it means to feel comfortable.**

Ask: • **What's your most comfortable spot, and what is it about this spot that makes it so comfortable?**

• **Who's a person who makes you feel comfortable, and what does this person do that gives you comfort?**

• **What does God do to comfort us?**

Say: **Let's take a look at Scripture to learn more about this.**

Have kids form four groups, and give each group a Bible, a poster board, markers, and craft supplies. Assign each group one of the following Scripture verses to look up and read.

Group 1: Romans 15:4

Group 2: 2 Corinthians 1:3

Group 3: Isaiah 51:3

Group 4: Nahum 1:7

Say: **Read your verse in your groups, and answer these two questions:**

• **What does this verse say God wants to do for us?**

• **What's something God wants us to do?**

After you've answered the questions, work together to create a picture that explains your Scripture verse.

Give kids 10 minutes; then have groups take turns explaining their verses, drawings, and findings.

Say: **Like a good shepherd, God keeps us from harm, offering us protection and comfort. And just like David, who wrote the 23rd Psalm, the more we trust in God's love and protection, the more comfort we receive. But we can take even greater comfort than David because we know God loves us so much that he sent us Jesus, who loved us enough to die for us.**

 (10 minutes)
Shields Up
This craft reminds us how God's Word, Jesus, protects and comforts us.

Give each child a copy of the "Jesus, Our Shepherd" handout on page 74, and set out an assortment of ink pads and pens.

Say: **Just as a rod and staff sound like odd things to give us comfort, not many people would have imagined that a cross where someone died could be comforting, either. God is very good to use everything possible to protect and comfort us.**

To help remind us of the way Jesus our shepherd protected every single one of us, each of you will ink your thumb, put your thumbprint on your handout and on every other person's handout, and write your first name under it. I'll give you enough time so that you can each collect prints from everyone in our group. Then add details to make a sheep out of each thumbprint. Gather the kids when they've all finished, and give them hand wipes.

Ask: • **What's something that makes you different, besides your thumbprint?**

• **Why do you think God made each one of us to be unique?**

• **How can this experience remind you that God loves you as a unique person?**

• **Why do you think Jesus loves you so much?**

| HOME AGAIN PRAYER | (up to 5 minutes) |

Say: **We've talked today about the many ways that God protects us from harm. Now for a few moments, close your eyes and picture some of the people and things God has provided to comfort and protect you. As you picture each person or thing, thank God for this. Begin now and we'll all thank God silently.**

After a few moments, pray: **God, thank you for protecting us in so many ways. We thank you for your comforting presence and your constant care and love. In Jesus' name. Amen.**

A Feast for Us

Pathway Point: God surprises us with blessings.

In-Focus Verse: "You prepare a feast for me in the presence of my enemies" (Psalm 23:5a).

Travel Itinerary

Imagine setting up a banquet in the middle of a battlefield. The picture of God preparing a meal for us while we're surrounded by enemies is vivid and unusual. People in Bible times probably understood this verse as a means of showing up a world that didn't believe in Yahweh. Constantly attacked and reviled for their faith, God's people had to hold onto God's assurance of his blessings and presence, no matter how dire or hopeless the situation might seem. God did and does confound the world by blessing his people in miraculous, unexplainable ways and places. Today we can also see this verse as more than proof or justification for our faith. We can hold onto the promise of God's presence, the hope of God meeting our needs, and the powerlessness of anyone or anything to take away these blessings.

 The experiences in this book have been designed for multi-age groups. Select from the experiences, or adapt them as needed for your kids.

| DEPARTURE PRAYER | (up to 5 minutes)

In this science experiment, children will complete a task that has an unexpected outcome.

 **Items to Pack:** 3x5 cards, pens, hand mirror

Have kids stand in two lines, each line facing the other. Say: **We're going to try a science experiment with a partner, so pair up with the person across from you.**

Give each child a 3x5 card and pen. Instruct each child to hold the index card against his or her forehead.

Say: **Using the pen, write your partner's name on the card from left to right while watching that person write your name.**

Have kids sit in a circle, and show them how to hold their cards up to the hand mirror so they can read the names they wrote backwards. After kids have passed the mirror around the circle, have kids find partners.

Say: **It probably came as a surprise to find it's so hard to write backwards!**

TOUR GUIDE TIP

If all the children in your group can't spell, ask the group to write the first five letters of the alphabet in order or the numbers one through five, so everyone can successfully write backwards.

Items to Pack: Bible, plastic bin, plastic utensils, paper plates, napkins, blindfolds

SCENIC ROUTE →

Give kids each a paper plate and have them draw a picture of the food they'd most like to have if God were serving them a feast. Then have kids take turns explaining their drawings and naming unlikely places where God could serve them, such as in a roller coaster, an elevator, or the middle of a classroom.

Ask • **When have you been surprised by something good that's happened to you?**

• **What's a not-so-good surprise that's happened to you?**

• **How can our faith in God's goodness help us when we have not-so-good surprises?**

Say: **God's blessings are all around us at every moment of our lives, but just as we needed the mirror to see the names we wrote, we sometimes need help to recognize God's blessings. Today's verse from the 23rd Psalm says, "You prepare a feast for me in the presence of my enemies."** **God surprises us with blessings in unexpected ways and unexpected places.**

Let's pray: **Dear God, sometimes we get worried when things don't turn out the way we want. Sometimes we feel confused because we don't understand why unexpected things happen. No matter where we are or what happens, we thank you for being with us and for blessing us. In Jesus' name. Amen.**

1st STOP DISCOVERY (15 minutes)

Table Setting Surprise

Kids will set a table with plates, napkins, and plastic utensils—in a surprising way—and talk about how to recognize God's unexpected blessings.

Bring out a plastic bin containing paper plates, napkins, and plastic utensils, and tell kids they're going to help you set the table.

Say: **In order to have a feast, we need to get ready. Let's set the table with these plates, utensils, and napkins. First I'll demonstrate how to do it. We usually put the fork on the left side of the plate, like this, and the knife and spoon on the right side. The napkin usually goes under the fork, like this.**

Say: **Now it's your turn to set a place...but oh, wait, let's make this a bit more challenging. How about a relay race? We'll see which team can finish first.** Have kids form two teams and line up relay-style about 5 feet away from the table. If you have a large group, set out multiple bins and form more teams.

Say: **Wait, I've got another idea: Let's do this blindfolded.** Give the first person in each team's line a blindfold. **When I say, "go," walk toward the table, find the bin, and then take out the items you need for your place setting. Create your place setting on the table, remove your**

blindfold, put your items back into the bin, and quickly pass the blindfold to the next team member.

Give kids enough time so everyone has a chance to do a table setting.

Ask: • **What was difficult about this experience?**

• **How would this experience have been different if you didn't know what items to look for in the bin? if I hadn't demonstrated how to set the table?**

• **How does knowing what to look for help us recognize God's blessings?**

• **What are some areas of life where we can be on the lookout for God's blessings?**

• **What can help us take off our "blindfolds" and see the good things God is doing for us?**

Have kids form pairs, and discuss these questions: • **When are times that your family invites special people to your home or serves special food?**

• **Why do you think we seem to have rules about special meals, such as when, where, and whom we invite to eat with us?**

Say: **God doesn't follow our rules or think like we do. ◗God surprises us with blessings in unexpected places. God sees possibilities to show us love in all situations and does so for all people.**

(15 minutes)
Leftover Blessings

Kids will read about a surprising feast to learn how God hears and responds to our needs wherever we are.

Say: **The Bible tells us about many times that ◗God surprised people with blessings. Let's use our Bibles now to find out about one of these times.**

Have kids form groups of four and read John 6:1-15. After they've had time to read, ask them to discuss the following questions in their groups. After each question invite groups to share their answers with the rest of the children.

• **Tell about a time you were in a situation where you had to share something and you weren't sure if there'd be enough for everyone.**

• **What would you have been thinking when you learned Jesus was attempting to feed everyone with just a little bit of food?**

• **Why do you think Jesus gave the people more food than they needed?**

Stay close at hand so you can gently guide kids if they need help moving toward the table.

FUN FACT

In addition to the theme of a good shepherd, Psalm 23 also includes the theme of a good host. In this case, the good host provides all that his honored guest might want, even if doing so caused him to face danger.

Items to Pack: Bibles, colorful copier paper or scrapbooking paper, markers

If you have access to gadgets, bring in a GPS locator and show kids the electronic listing of stores around them. Count them and then talk about the countless places God blesses us because God is located everywhere.

SCENIC ROUTE →
Challenge kids to research what happens to leftover food from local restaurants. If restaurants donate food to local shelters, soup kitchens, or food banks, have kids write letters of appreciation.

Items to Pack: Bible, graham crackers, pretzel sticks, trail mix (without raisins or nuts), round vanilla cookies, frosting, table settings from 1st Stop Discovery

If these snacks conflict with the allergy or wellness policies at your church, use the following alternatives: mozzarella or celery sticks, rice crackers, spreadable cream cheese, and thin carrot slices.

• **How grateful are you for the food you have to eat each day? for the leftovers you sometimes need to eat?**

• **What can you do for those who have less food to eat than you have?**

Hand out paper and markers to each child. Have kids fold their papers in half, and then in half again to create a note card.

Say: **This week we're learning to look for the surprising ways that God blesses us. Sometimes, though, we can overlook the ways God blesses us in the ordinary daily circumstances of our lives. Let's take a few minutes to think about some of these everyday blessings and write to our loving Shepherd, giving thanks for those blessings and asking God to help us pay closer attention to the many good things we receive.**

Encourage kids to take their notes home as reminders to look for God's blessings in the coming week.

(10 minutes)
Food for Thought

Children will use food items to tell the story of Paul urging his enemies to eat in the midst of an upcoming shipwreck.

Have children wash their hands before this experience.

Say: **We're about to go on an adventure.** Open the Bible to Acts 27 and show the children. **This adventure is from the book of Acts, a very exciting book about the early church. To tell this story and help us remember it, we're going to use some "feast" food.** Give each child a paper plate. Then hand out eight pretzel sticks, one graham cracker, and a spoonful of frosting to each child.

Say: **At the beginning of chapter 27 in Acts, Paul was in prison, and the people who arrested him decided he needed to go on trial far away. So they put him on a boat, and the boat went to sea. Using our knives, let's spread the frosting along the outer edge of the graham cracker to start making a boat. Then let's build up the sides of the boat by laying down pretzels on each edge and "gluing" them together with a bit more frosting.** (Pause.)

Say: **It was going to be a long, hard journey, so the sailors packed lots of food and supplies. Let's put our trail mix inside the boat and**

set the filled boat on our plates. Place a spoonful of trail mix on each child's plate. (Pause.)

Ask: • **How do you think Paul felt being a prisoner on a boat going far away from home?**

• **When was a time you felt something like this?**

Say: **It got even worse for Paul. A terrible storm came. This storm lasted days and days until everyone became certain the boat would sink. No one could eat. The storm blotted out the sun and the stars. The sailors tried to make the boat lighter by throwing things overboard. People felt hopeless. Take the trail mix out of your boat and put it back on your plate to make your boat lighter.** (Pause.)

Ask: • **What kinds of things sometimes happen that can make you feel like you're caught in a bad storm?**

• **What are some negative ideas or attitudes that you could "throw overboard" to help you feel better during a rough time?**

• **How does your trust in God help you at such times?**

• **What are some ways you can help others when they feel worried or without hope?**

Say: **Then one night an angel of God appeared to Paul. The angel told Paul not to be afraid—the boat would be shipwrecked, but God would keep all the people safe. The next day Paul gave God's message to everyone and said he believed it. The storm lasted 14 days, and then as morning dawned, even though the boat was still being tossed around, Paul urged all the people to eat. He knew the boat was going to be shipwrecked, but he knew that God would take care of them. Turn your boat over now to make a table.**

Ask: • **How do you think you would've felt if you were on the boat when Paul shared God's message?**

• **Why is it so hard to expect God's blessings during a difficult time?**

• **What could someone do that would bring you encouragement when you don't see God's blessings?**

• **Who do you know who needs encouragement right now, and how can you give it?**

Hand out the cookies. Say: **Let's each put a plate on our tables and use frosting to hold it in place. Then we'll put a bit of frosting on top of the plate and add trail mix for our feast. Paul had faith that God would bless him in this unexpected place. A fierce storm and enemies**

SCENIC ROUTE →

Setting up food items in different places around the room will allow kids to "travel" through the story. Designate the first station or stop with pretzels, graham crackers, and frosting as the ship's port, where kids will build their boats. Place trail mix at the second station to represent the spot in the ocean where the crew throws items overboard. Place vanilla wafers at the third station as the spot out at sea where Paul urged the people to eat.

TOUR GUIDE TIP

Some children have food allergies that can be dangerous. Know your children, and consult with parents about allergies their children may have. Also, read food labels carefully, as hidden ingredients can cause allergy-related problems.

SCENIC ROUTE →

Although using food to tell the story is recommended, it's possible to tell the story using clay or paper shaped in long strips or rolls, squares, circles, and small rectangles.

Items to Pack: Bibles, copies of "Disciple's Ship" handout on page 82, tape, scissors, markers

surrounded him, but it didn't matter. Before he ate, he took bread, gave thanks to God before everyone, broke off a piece of bread, and ate it. Then they all ate. The boat was shipwrecked—but all the people were saved. Let's pray, too, before we eat our feast.

Pray: **God, thank you for your love and grace. Thank you for surprising us with blessings. We praise you for giving us feasts to meet our needs, no matter where we are. In Jesus' name we pray. Amen.**

Have kids help clean up after they've finished eating.

 (10 minutes)

Disciple's Ship

This craft reminds children to look for surprising blessings everywhere.

Have kids sit at a table, and give them each a copy of the "Disciple's Ship" handout on page 82 and markers. Take out a Bible and turn to the 23rd Psalm.

Say: **In Acts 27 we learned Paul had faith that 🌐 God surprises us with blessings in unexpected places. When he urged his enemies to eat with him in the middle of a great storm, Paul might have even been thinking of the 23rd Psalm in the Old Testament. No matter what the situation or who stands against us, God cares for *us*, too. Write on the table of food in your handout some of the ways God has blessed you.**

When kids are finished, give them scissors and tape. Have them cut out the table of food. Next have them fold the tabs and the dotted line in the middle of the table and then tape the tabs to the lines on the boat.

Say: **Part of discipleship is setting an example for others. Paul, a prisoner with guards around him, was in the storm with everyone else. Yet all these powerful people and the raging storm didn't bother Paul. He knew about God's power.**

Ask: • **What are some ways we can show that we know God is more powerful than anything or anyone?**

• **How do we help others by showing our faith?**

Say: **Paul did even more than show bravery. Paul encouraged the people who were holding him prisoner. He told them God would take care of them, too, and encouraged them to eat. The most surprising thing is that he did this in the middle of a storm just as the boat looked like it might sink.**

Ask: • **Why did Paul help his enemies?**

• **What blessings do you think God wants us to give those who aren't our friends?**

Say: **We don't want to have enemies because we know God loves everyone, but sometimes there are people we don't get along with. Remember, though, that** **God surprises us with blessings, so maybe if we treat our "enemies" kindly, as Paul did, we'd find even more surprising blessings in unlikely places and people.**

Have kids place their "Disciple's Ships" in their Travel Journals.

HOME AGAIN PRAYER (up to 5 minutes)

Ahead of time, write each child's name on a sticky note, and hide it somewhere in the room.

Say: **God surprises us with blessings, but we need to be on the lookout for these blessings. Look around the room now for a sticky note with your name on it. When you find it, come and place it on the wall so we can remember the blessings we've been given in each other. When you've found your name, you can help others if they want help.**

After all the kids have found their names, say: **God doesn't hide blessings like I hid your sticky notes. We just forget to look for his blessings—especially in surprising places.**

Let's pray: God, as we rush from place to place, help us to pause and look for the blessings you surprise us with in unexpected places. Thank you for being everywhere with us, blessing us with your presence. In Jesus' name we pray. Amen.

Items to Pack: sticky notes, pen

TOUR GUIDE TIP

Don't have room for this experience? Let all kids work together to build a house of cards, naming places to look for blessings and seeing how high the tower can get.

← Tent fold in center

Fold
Tab
Behind

Fold
Tab
Behind

← Glue tabs to lines so Paul is on top
but people are still visible →

Anointed With Oil

Pathway Point: God heals us.

In-Focus Verse: "You honor me by anointing my head with oil" (Psalm 23:5b).

Travel Itinerary

In ancient Israel, people used oil to promote health; it also symbolized honor. Kings, such as Saul and David, were anointed with oil, and hosts anointed their guests' heads with oil on feasts and other special occasions. The image of being treated as a special, honored guest reflects the sense of belonging and healing that God offers each of us. Even as the beginning verses of the 23rd Psalm focus on us as the sheep of God's flock, the later verses invite us to a more honored and exalted status within God's abundant care.

DEPARTURE PRAYER	(up to 5 minutes)

Children will learn about the use of oil in ancient Israel and then use oil to bless each other.

Ahead of time, pour a few ounces of vegetable oil into a small bowl.

Have kids sit in a circle. Open the Bible and say: This week our verse from the 23d Psalm says: **"You honor me by anointing my head with oil." Anointing means placing oil on someone for a special reason. In Bible times, people used oil to heal people and sometimes to honor them. Both Saul and David were anointed with oil to show that God wanted them to become kings. When guests came to people's homes on special occasions, hosts would anoint their heads with oil to show honor.**

Ask: • **What are some ways we welcome people as guests in our homes?**

• **What makes you feel special when you visit someone's home?**

• **How does God treat you like someone special?**

Say: **We don't anoint people in the same way they did in Bible times, but they also used oil as a medicine to bring healing, and it can still be used to help heal our skin. We can also use oil as a way to express God's blessing and ask for healing. Though this oil heals**

> **TOUR GUIDE TIP**
>
> The experiences in this book have been designed for multi-age groups. Select from the experiences, or adapt them as needed.

> **Items to Pack:** Bible, small bowl, vegetable oil, paper towels, newspapers

> **TOUR GUIDE TIP**
>
> Due to allergies, make sure the kind of vegetable oil you use is safe for all the kids to touch or be around.

> **FUN FACT**
>
> Shepherds in ancient Israel used oil to anoint the sheep. It not only healed their wounds but also kept away flies, mosquitoes, and gnats.

TOUR GUIDE TIP

If you have the opportunity, show children different types of vegetable oils and point out that olive oil was the most commonly used kind in Bible times.

FUN FACT

Lanolin, the oil taken from sheep's wool, is used to make lotions that keep skin healthy, to make waterproofing wax to protect stainless steel, and even to make Vitamin D3.

SCENIC ROUTE →

For a less active option, have kids start naming times they've been sick or hurt and gotten better. Each time kids name a time, pour a bit of oil into a measuring cup. Do this until the cup is full or kids run out of examples.

on the outside, 🌑God heals us on the inside.

We're going to pass some oil around our circle. When the bottle comes to you, dip your finger into the oil and place a dot of oil on the forehead of the person next to you, saying, "God's love heals you, [person's name]." Begin by placing oil on the forehead of the child to your left. When everyone's been blessed, close in prayer.

Pray: **God, we thank you for honoring us and healing us with your love. We praise you for doing so much for us. Help us to learn more about your care so we can tell others about it. In Jesus' name we pray. Amen.**

1st STOP DISCOVERY (10 minutes)
Feeling Better
Kids will play a variation of Musical Chairs to recall times they've received healing.

Make a circle of chairs, with one less chair than you have children, and choose someone to be "It."

Say: **We're going to play a quick game of Musical Chairs to help us remember all the times God has made us better when we've been sick or hurt. The person who's It will stand inside the circle of chairs, and everyone else will take a seat. Then It will call out some way he or she has ever been sick or hurt—this can be anything from a mosquito bite to a broken arm. If you've ever been sick or hurt in the same way, you need to jump up and move to another chair. It will try to sit down, too, and whoever doesn't have a new seat will be the new It. If no one's ever been sick or hurt in the same way, It calls again, naming something different. Got it? Okay, let's go!**

Let kids play for five minutes. Then say: **What a loving God we have to bless us with bodies that can heal and bounce back when we get sick or hurt. We know sometimes this can take awhile, though.**

Ask: • **What's the worst time of being sick that you've experienced?**

• **When you feel sick, what helps you feel better?**

• **When someone else is sick, what's something you can do to help that person feel better?**

Say: **We know it's true, too, that sometimes people don't always heal. Right now think about someone you know who's really sick and needs God's healing.**

Ask: • **Where's God when someone is sick and doesn't get better?**

• **What can help us trust God when something like this happens?**

Say: **While oil just heals us on the outside,** **God heals us on the inside.**

Ask: • **How can we help each other remember that God can heal us on the inside as well as on the outside?**

Say: **When we first looked at our Bible verse, it might have seemed hard to understand how being anointed with oil makes us feel honored or healed, but oil represents God's special care that comes to us whenever we need it.**

(15 minutes)
God's Band-Aids

Kids will learn about the many ways that God heals us.

Have kids form four groups, and give each group a Bible, markers, and a large sheet of newsprint.

Say: **Now we're going to take a closer look at more ways that God wants to heal us. In your groups find Isaiah 61:1-3 and read it together. Then have one person in your group lie down on the paper so you can trace an outline of his or her body. On your papers, either inside or outside the body outline, write or draw the ways this Scripture verse says** **God heals us. You have five minutes.**

When kids are finished, have each group hold up its drawing and use it to re-tell Isaiah 61:1-3, showing the ways that God heals us.

Ask: • **Which ways that God brings healing surprised you most?**

• **What other feelings do we sometimes have inside us that God wants to heal?**

• **What are some ways that people suffer when they're poor?**

• **How can we help God bring these people "good news"?**

Give each child an adhesive bandage and a pen. Say: **Now pick one way God heals us out of all your answers, and write it on the bandage so you'll remember it. You can wear the bandage if you like— just choose an easy place to remove it later, such as the inside of your wrist.**

(10 minutes)
Blessed and Sent

Kids will learn that just like the disciples, we're called to bring healing, too.

Give each child a sheet of construction paper and markers.

TOUR GUIDE TIP Sometimes children may bring up difficult topics about healing. If you're dealing with children who've faced a death in the family or disability, reassure them of God's love and God's desire to heal us from the pain of grief or anger.

Items to Pack: Bibles, 4 sheets of large paper or newsprint, markers, pens, adhesive bandages

TOUR GUIDE TIP Advise children not to place band-aids on clothing. If they're going to wear their band-aids, tell kids to place them on their skin, quickly remove them, and then put them back on. When reapplied the band-aids will be less painful to remove.

Items to Pack: Bible, wastebasket, construction paper, markers

Say: **In our adventure today we're going to hear about the disciples taking a trip. But first, fold your paper in half, and let's pretend it's a suitcase. Think about going on a trip, and on the inside of your paper, draw all the things you need to take with you on a trip. You'll only have a few minutes, so try to pick the most important items.**

Ask: • **What things did you include?**

• **What's the most important thing you included?**

• **What would happen on a trip if you forgot this most important thing?**

• **What do you think the disciples would pack if Jesus sent them out on a trip?**

Say: **You might think Jesus would go with his disciples, but he didn't. He sent the disciples out with a partner, but they had to go without him.**

Ask: • **Why do you think Jesus didn't go with them?**

• **Why do you think he sent the disciples in pairs?**

Say: **Even though the disciples hadn't learned a lot from Jesus yet, he told them to share what they knew. He said something even more surprising—he said they had to go on their trip without food, extra clothes, or money. All they could take were the clothes they were wearing, a staff, and the sandals on their feet.**

So crumple up your paper suitcase now, and toss it into the waste-basket like a basketball. If you miss, you can throw it again from wherever it landed. When you've gotten rid of your luggage, come back and sit in a circle by me.

When everyone's back, say: **Listen now while I read Mark 6:6-13.**

Read the passage, and then ask: • **How would you feel if you had to travel somewhere and couldn't take anything with you?**

• **Why do you think Jesus told the disciples to do this?**

• **Why did Jesus send his disciples out to heal people instead of going himself?**

• **Who are the people in our world who are hurting and need healing? in our school? in our families?**

• **What kinds of things can we do to make people feel better?**

• **How can we show others what we've learned about the way God's love brings healing?**

Afterward say: **God uses everything to bring healing to a world that needs his love. ◐God heals us, and then we're able to bring healing**

86

to others. **The disciples didn't need anything but God's love to bring healing to people. We need to trust God just as the disciples did and know that we can bring healing to each other because of God's love.**

SOUVENIRS (10 minutes)
God's Love Heals

This will be a make-one/give-one craft, so each child and a friend will have a reminder that ⬤ God heals us.

Items to Pack: Bible, copies of the "God's Love Brings Healing" handout on page 89, scissors, colored pencils, cotton balls, vegetable oil, small bowl, glue, 2 resealable plastic snack bags for each child

Ahead of time, for each child, dip a cotton ball in oil and place it in a resealable plastic snack bag. Set out scissors, glue, cotton balls, and colored pencils, and place a few ounces of vegetable oil in a small bowl. Give each child a copy of the "God's Love Brings Healing" handout on page 89.

Have kids each cut out the award ribbons and the two extra circles. Then ask kids to write in each award ribbon's circle one way that ⬤ God heals us. Then have kids place glue around the edges of the extra circles and place them on top of the award ribbon circles, so their messages are covered.

Say: **Today we're going to use some oil to show how God's love brings us healing.**

Then hand out the cotton balls, and have each child dip a cotton ball lightly into the vegetable oil.

Say: **Even though we can't see the words you wrote too well right now, the oil will fix this if you rub it over the circle on one of your award ribbons.** Pause while children do this.

Just as oil made the message visible, what we do for others can help make God's love visible. We can be used by God to help bring healing to others.

You have a message you need to share with a friend. I'm going to give you a resealable plastic bag with a cotton ball dipped in oil. Give your extra award ribbon to a friend, and rub the cotton ball over the circle to show this person your message.

Have kids each place their award ribbon in a resealable plastic bag and then into their Travel Journals. Give children each a bag with an oily cotton ball to take with their extra award ribbon.

SCENIC ROUTE Turn the award ribbons into refrigerator magnets by cutting a magnetic-tape strip into small pieces and attaching a piece to the back of each award ribbon.

HOME AGAIN PRAYER (up to 5 minutes)

Children will ask for God's healing.

Have kids form pairs.

Say: **For our closing prayer, let's ask God to heal us. With your partner, talk about those times you need God's love and healing most, such as when you're sad, mad, lonely, or scared. When you've finished, take turns saying to each other, "May God's love heal you."**

When kids are done, say: **God loves us so much that he wants to heal us in every possible way. Sometimes the healing God does is to make us feel better inside or to teach us to trust him more. God also welcomes each of us as his special guest. He pours out his blessings on us like oil—blessings that are too wonderful and too many to count.**

Let's pray silently for God to heal us now.

After a few moments of silence, pray: **God, thank you for bringing us healing in so many ways. You make us feel loved and honored. Thank you for loving us so much. In Jesus' name. Amen.**

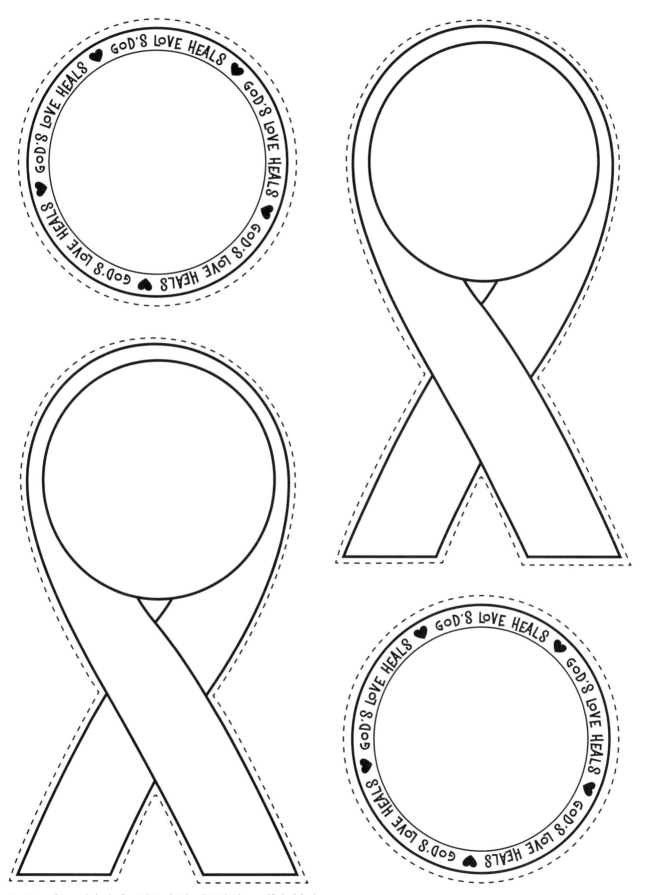

GOD'S LOVE HEALS GOD'S LOVE HEALS GOD'S LOVE HEALS GOD'S LOVE HEALS

GOD'S LOVE HEALS GOD'S LOVE HEALS GOD'S LOVE HEALS

Overflowing With Blessings

Pathway Point:  God gives us good things.

In-Focus Verse: "My cup overflows with blessings" (Psalm 23:5c).

TOUR GUIDE TIP

The experiences in this book have been designed for multi-age groups. Select from the experiences, or adapt them as needed.

Travel Itinerary

The children you teach may have a hard time differentiating between what they need versus what they want. Kids are bombarded with media advertisements that shout what kids just shouldn't have to live without—the newest video games, clothes, toys, and even electronic equipment.

In the face of media and peer pressure, kids may be so surrounded by this consumer culture that they fail to notice the blessings God showers on them every day.

Use this adventure to help kids see how God not only takes care of their daily needs but also provides the lasting and nurturing blessings of love, family, and the offer of eternal life.

Items to Pack:
magazines, scissors

| **DEPARTURE PRAYER** | (up to 10 minutes) |

Gather kids together in a circle on the floor.

Say: **Today we're talking about how God gives us good things. Let's discover what kinds of good things we all enjoy.** Set out scissors and several kid-appropriate magazines. Have kids each cut out a picture of a good thing he or she enjoys. Cut out a picture for yourself.

Say: **When you're finished, bring your picture back to the circle.**

When everyone has returned to the circle, ask: • **What was it like coming up with a picture of a good thing in your life?**

• **After this experience, how would you define a "good thing"?**

Say: **There are tons of good things in this world to enjoy. And it's important to remember that ⬤ God gives us good things. Let's thank God for giving us all kinds of good things.**

We'll go around the circle in this prayer. I'll start by thanking God for the good thing I cut out; then I'll place my picture in the center of the circle.

Begin the prayer by thanking God for whatever you cut out, and then place

TOUR GUIDE TIP

If you'd rather not gather magazines, let each child write about or draw a good thing he or she enjoys.

your picture, facing up, on the floor in the center of the circle. Go around the circle until everyone has prayed and placed a picture in the circle. Then end the prayer by thanking God for all the good things he gives us every day.

 (20 minutes)

Filled to Overflowing

Kids will do an experiment where they discover that their lives overflow with good things from God.

Items to Pack: stones, permanent markers, towel or paper towels, jar of water

Fill a jar to the top with water. Set the jar on a towel or paper towels. Set out the stones and permanent markers.

Say: **Let's talk a little more about how 🌎God gives us good things. It's pretty easy to see the good things in our lives—physical objects that we can see and touch and play with. Grab a stone and write on it one of your favorite *physical* good things in your life. Maybe you'll write "game" for your favorite video game or "shoes" for the new pair you just got.**

Pause to let kids write.

Say: **Now grab another stone and write on it one of your favorite *less-physical* good things in your life. Maybe you'll write "love" for the way your family loves you or "sun" for the bright sunshine you see every day.**

Pause as kids write. Then gather kids and their stones in a circle around the jar of water.

Help younger kids differentiate between physical objects such as toys and more abstract blessings such as love or protection.

Say: **We'll go around the circle twice. The first time, say what you wrote on your first stone and then drop it into the water. Then we'll go around again, and you can say what you wrote on your second stone and drop that one into the water, too. Pay attention to what happens to the water.**

Go around the circle twice, letting kids drop in their stones after saying what they wrote.

Ask: • **What happened to the water as you dropped in your stones?**
• **How is that like the good things from God in your life?**

Say: **The water overflowed as you dropped in the stones. It's the same way with good things from God. Listen to what the Bible says as part of Psalm 23: "My cup overflows with blessings."**

God gives us so many good things that they overflow in our lives.

Ask: • **Why do you think we sometimes forget about the many**

Remind kids that permanent markers really are "permanent." You might want to provide simple paint smocks for younger kids.

good things that God gives us?

• **What can we do to help us remember these good things every day?**

Say: **Even when we may not feel like our cups are overflowing with blessings, they are. Just think about it—we have shelter, we have food, we have clean water, we have families, we have clothes, we have friends, we have toys, we have cars, we have sunlight, we have heat, we have flowers, we have...well, you get the picture! There are just so many good things to name. This week, take time every day to look for the good things God gives you.**

But right now, let's meet someone who seriously needed some good things from God.

(20 minutes)

Jars of Joy

Kids will learn that we can trust God to give us good things even when situations seem hopeless.

Have kids form pairs.

Say: **Let's try an experiment before we dive into the Bible.**

Choose a pair to come forward, and have the partner who's wearing the most blue sit in the chair.

Say: **It might sound like an easy thing to get up out of that chair. But I'll prove otherwise.**

Have the seated child sit up straight in the chair with his or her lower back touching the back of the chair. Have the child place his or her feet flat on the floor, and place both hands in his or her lap.

Touch the child's forehead with an index finger, applying gentle pressure. Tell the child to stand up without using his or her hands or arms for leverage. The child won't be able to rise.

Let the seated child get up and perform the experiment with the other partner. Then let each pair have a turn. When everyone has had a chance to sit in the chair, call kids back together.

Have partners discuss the following questions. After each question, ask kids to share their answers with the rest of the group.

Ask: • **What was it like trying to stand up?**

• **How is that like facing a difficult problem in life?**

• **Tell your partner about a time you felt like you faced a problem that couldn't be solved.**

Items to Pack: Bibles, paper, scissors, markers, straight-back chair, scrap paper, paper cups

TOUR GUIDE TIP

The trick to this experiment is having the seated person sit all the way back in a straight chair, with both feet flat on the floor and both hands in his or her lap.

Say: **Sometimes it really can feel as though a problem has no solution. That's exactly what happened to a woman in the Bible. Let's find out more.**

Open your Bible to 2 Kings 4:1-7, and show kids the passage. Say: **This woman had a terrible problem, and she didn't see any way out. Let's see what that was like.**

Give each person a sheet of paper. Set out markers for kids to share.

Say: **Draw a picture of your family. Include your parents and your brothers and sisters. You can even include your grandparents—and your dog if you want. Put the people you love in your picture.**

When kids have finished drawing, have them form new pairs. Give partners a few minutes to show and explain their pictures. Invite a few kids to show their pictures to the entire group.

Say: **Now imagine that two of the people you drew were no longer part of your family.**

Ask: • **What would it be like in your family if these two people weren't there?**

• **How would you react if that situation were really happening in your family?**

Say: **Perhaps some of us have already experienced something like this because of death or divorce or someone moving away. The woman in the Bible today was facing a similar problem.**

Read aloud 2 Kings 4:1-2.

Ask: • **What would you have done if you were this woman?**

Say: **Elisha was a prophet of God, and he had an idea. By the way, God used prophets to give his messages to the people. And a "flask" is kind of like a jar.**

Okay, now I'll need your help to tell what happened to the woman and her sons.

Gather kids near a table in your room. At one end of the table, place a supply of scrap paper. Place a supply of paper cups at another spot in your room.

Say: **I'll read what happened in the Bible, and you can re-enact the action, okay? I'll tell you what to do.** Read aloud 2 Kings 4:3. **Quick! We need as many empty jars as possible. Uh-oh, I don't see any jars. But I do see empty cups. We'll use those. Hurry! Run over to the cups, and each bring one back to the table.** In an urgent voice, encourage kids to keep bringing empty cups to the table.

SCENIC ROUTE This may bring out some areas of need in kids' lives. Be prepared to stop and talk more in depth if kids seem willing. Reassure kids that God loves them and is aware of their needs. Also offer to talk afterward with any child who may be struggling with hardship. Look for ways your church might help.

TOUR GUIDE TIP If some kids only have two people in their pictures, have them imagine what it would be like if there were only one person.

Okay, good work. Let's see what happened next. Read aloud 2 Kings 4:4. **Olive oil...olive oil—I don't see any olive oil. Ah, but I do see some scrap paper. Let's wad up the scrap paper and pretend that it's olive oil. Hurry up, start filling up those cups!** Urge kids to wad up scrap paper, fill the cups with paper wads, and set them on the floor across the room. When all the cups have been filled and moved, gather kids together.

Say: **Whew! Great work! Let's find out more about what happened in the Bible.** Read aloud 2 Kings 4:5. **So far, so good—we did just what the woman's sons did.** Pause and then look back in the Bible. **Let's see. It says here that the woman said, "Bring me another jar." Do we have any more jars?** Pause as kids look for more cups. **No more? Okay, that's just what happened in the Bible. One of the sons said, "There isn't any more!" And then the olive oil stopped flowing.**

Ask: • **In the beginning of this Bible account, the woman said she had just one flask of oil left. So how were they able to fill all those jars with oil?**

• **What do you think they did with all that oil?**

Say: **Listen to what happened.** Read aloud 2 Kings 4:7.

Say: **What might have happened if the woman had doubted Elisha and not done what he said?**

• **Why do we sometimes doubt God's good plans for us?**

Say: **God gives us good things. He always loves us and always knows what's best. We may not understand situations sometimes, but we can always trust that God has good plans for us—plans that include good things.**

(10 minutes)

ADVENTURES IN GROWING

Say It Yourself

Kids will discover other psalms David wrote and then write psalms of their own.

Say: **Today we've been learning the part of the 23rd Psalm that says, "My cup overflows with blessings." David wrote this psalm to show how good God is. Let's look at some other psalms David wrote.**

Have kids form four groups, and give each group at least one Bible. Assign each group one of the following psalms:

• Psalm 16   • Psalm 70

• Psalm 86   • Psalm 139

Items to Pack: Bibles, paper, pencils

Say: **In your group, read the psalm I gave you. Then together, think about what David said to God. In some psalms he praised God. In some, he asked God for help. In all of them, he told God how he felt about him.**

After your discussion, work together to write your own psalm to God. Think about how knowing that **God gives us good things can change your life this week. Then write a psalm to God saying how you feel. I'll pass out paper and pencils while you get started.**

When kids have finished writing, invite a few kids to read what their group wrote. Say: **God gives us good things because he loves us—plain and simple. This week, no matter what you face, remember that, and remember that you can tell God anything, just as David did.**

TOUR GUIDE TIP Tell kids their psalms can be short, and they won't have to read them out loud unless they want to. Be ready to offer assistance, but only if needed.

SOUVENIRS → (10 minutes)
Blessing Reminders

This experience will provide a reminder of how God pours out his blessings in kids' lives.

Items to Pack: Bibles, copies of "My Cup Overflows" handout on page 97, pens, colored pencils, fine-tipped markers

Form pairs and give each pair a Bible; then have kids read today's verse from Psalm 23 with their partners: **"My cup overflows with blessings."**

Ask: • **What does this verse mean to you?**

• **How have you seen the truth of this verse in your life?**

Say: **God pours out his love and blessings in our lives, just as he made the olive oil pour out for the woman in the Bible.**

Give each child a copy of the "My Cup Overflows" handout on page 97. Set out pens, colored pencils, and fine-tipped markers for kids to share.

Say: **On the handout, you'll see four jars representing four different parts of your life. Above each jar draw a big drop of oil. Then write or draw on each drop a way God has blessed you in that area.**

When kids have finished writing and drawing, say: **Put your handouts into your Travel Journals to remind you that** **God gives us good things. Like the Bible says, our cups overflow with God's blessings. Let's thank God for all of the good things he gives us.**

<table>
<tr><td>

HOME AGAIN PRAYER

</td><td>

(10 minutes)

Use this experience to help kids remember to thank God for his blessings throughout the week.

</td></tr>
</table>

Have kids form pairs.

Say: **This week, let's remember that** **God gives us good things. This experience can help us do that.**

Let's have each pair make up a simple two-line rhyme that they can say when they see examples of God's goodness this week. Then we'll vote on which rhyme we like best, and we'll use it in our closing prayer. Here's my rhyme:

Thank you, God, for all good things.

Thank you for the love you bring.

Give kids a few minutes to compose their rhymes. Then have each pair present its creation. Let the class vote on which rhyme they like best, and then thank everyone for their contributions.

Form a circle. Say: **Let's all say the chosen rhyme together. Then I'll tell God one good thing I'm thankful for. We'll all say the rhyme again, and the next person in the circle will name a good thing he or she is thankful for. We'll say the rhyme again and continue going around the circle until everyone's shared.**

Close the prayer by thanking God for loving us so much, and for all the good things he gives us every day.

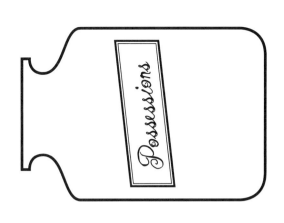

~~~~~~

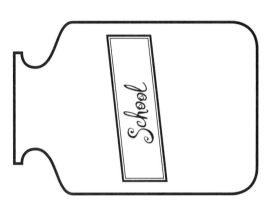

~~~~~~

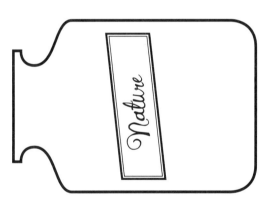

~~~~~~

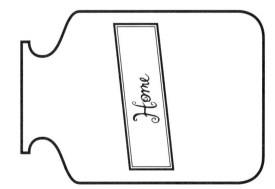

Unfailing Love

Pathway Point: God is always with us.

In-Focus Verse: "Surely your goodness and unfailing love will pursue me all the days of my life" (Psalm 23:6a).

Travel Itinerary

Often kids (and adults!) have the idea that a relationship with God requires constant action on the part of the person. If he or she just tries a little harder to be good, reads the Bible a little more, prays more often—then a deep relationship with God will result.

And these actions are all good things to do. But kids may fail to see God working in their lives. They may not realize that God is constantly pursuing them. That he fervently desires a lasting relationship with them—one that will last for eternity.

Use this adventure to help kids understand that God's love never fails, never ends, and never stops pursuing us.

TOUR GUIDE TIP

The experiences in this book have been designed for multi-age groups. Select from the experiences, or adapt them as needed.

DEPARTURE PRAYER (up to 5 minutes)

Bring kids together.

Say: **God is always with us. And to help us get started today, let's play a quick game.**

Choose one person to be "It," and explain that It will try to tag as many other people as possible before you call time. Start the game of Tag, and let kids play for about a minute. Call time, and choose another person to be It. Play several rounds. Then gather everyone together in a circle on the floor.

Ask: • **What was it like being chased by It in this game?**

Say: **In the game of Tag, It chases and tries to catch everyone else. In a way, God does the same thing. I'm not saying God chases us around like in a game of Tag, but God is always with us. And he wants very much for us to know and love him.**

Let's thank God for wanting to be with us.

Have kids spread out around the room and freeze. Explain that you'll start the active prayer by tagging another person and saying, "God wants to be with you." Then that person will say the same phrase as he or she tags someone else.

98

After kids have each tagged someone else, they'll move to the center of the room and form a circle.

When everyone has joined the circle, join hands. Pray: **God, thank you for loving us so much, and for wanting to always be with us. We love you. In Jesus' name. Amen.**

(10 minutes)
Me and My Shadow

Kids will use flashlights to discover that just like their shadows, God is always with them.

Bring kids together.

Say: **Let's discover more about how God is always with us.**

Have kids stand in a bunch in the center of the room. Give each person a flashlight. Turn off the lights, and make the room as dark as possible. Let kids experiment with the flashlights to make shadows on the walls. Don't guide them too much—a little free exploration time is fine.

After several minutes, gather kids around you. Say: **You made lots of cool shadows. Now I want you to make some more, but this time make your shadow do something on its own—not the same thing you're doing. Okay, make those new shadows!**

As kids try to make their shadows move independently, say things such as, "Come on, make your shadow move on its own" and "What's the matter with your shadow?"

After a few minutes, gather kids in a circle, and turn on the lights. Have kids turn off the flashlights.

Ask: • **What was it like trying to get your shadow to move on its own?**

• **Why did your shadow do everything you did?**

Say: **Your shadow sure stuck to you, didn't it? You couldn't get rid of it, no matter how you tried. It went everywhere with you.**

That's kind of how God is. God is always with us, everywhere we go. He loves us so much, he goes everywhere with us, and never leaves us all alone—kind of like a shadow.

Listen to today's verse from the 23rd Psalm: "Surely your goodness and unfailing love will pursue me all the days of my life."

Ask: • **What do you think this verse means?**

• **How do God's goodness and love remind you of a shadow?**

TOUR GUIDE TIP

If you have time, allow each child special time "on stage" to show off a shadow. That will make the second part of the activity where kids can't escape their shadows even more meaningful.

99

Say: **This verse says that God's goodness and love follow us all the days of our lives. God's goodness and love are like our shadows—they always follow us. I'm so thankful for that!**

Right now, let's find out about a guy in the Bible who learned the meaning of this verse in a big way.

 (20 minutes)
Let's See About Saul

This experience will teach kids that because of his great love, Jesus pursued Saul and changed his life, just as Jesus can do with us.

Open your Bible to Acts 9:1-20, and show kids the passage.

Say: **To start, let's play a game called Capture the Christians. That's pretty much what the guy in the Bible, Saul, was doing.**

Choose one person to be Saul, and everyone else will be the Christians. Explain that when you say, "go," the Christians will scatter around the room as Saul tries to tag them. But Saul may only hop. If Saul tags a Christian, that person must go to jail in a designated corner of the room. A Christian can't be tagged if he or she is hiding behind a solid object such as a chair, but a Christian can only hide for a count of five.

When everyone understands the rules, begin play. Play for several minutes; then call time and see how many Christians Saul was able to put in jail. Choose a new Saul, and play again.

After the game, gather kids around you.

Ask: • **What was it like being chased by Saul?**

• **What would it be like if someone were really trying to put you in jail for being a Christian?**

Say: **Well, that's exactly what happened in the Bible. This took place after Jesus had returned to heaven. Saul was mad that people still believed in Jesus—he thought they were all wrong. He wanted to punish them, so he tried to catch them and put them in jail, kind of like in our game.**

But then something amazing happened to Saul. Let's find out more.

Form four groups, and give each group a Bible, paper, and pencils. Set out newsprint and colored markers for kids to share.

Say: **In your group, you'll read the rest of the Bible passage, and then decide how to tell what happened to the rest of the group. You can write a newspaper story, you can act it out, you can present a TV**

Items to Pack: Bibles, paper, newsprint, pencils, colored markers

Explain that many Christians still suffer for their faith in Jesus. Pause for a quick prayer for Christians worldwide who still face persecution.

news show, you can write a song, you can draw a movie advertisement, or you can even create a reality show. The only rules are that you need to tell the rest of us what happened in the Bible in your own creative way.

Oh, and you'll only have seven minutes. Better get going!

Tell kids to read Acts 9:3-20, and base their presentations on that passage. Circulate around the room to offer kids help and ideas, if necessary. After six minutes, give groups a one-minute warning. After another minute, call time.

Let groups take turns presenting the Bible passage. Lead everyone in applause after each presentation. Then ask groups to go back to the Bible and read the passage again. Ask them to see if any important facts were left out of the presentations. After a few minutes, let each group share its findings.

Say: **Thanks for that detective work. I think we now have a pretty good idea of what happened to Saul. But I still have some questions.** Have kids discuss the following questions in their groups. After each question, invite kids to share their insights.

Ask: • **Explain which person in this Bible passage you feel you're the most like.**

• **Saul had been saying some bad things about Jesus. Why do you think Jesus still wanted to have a relationship with Saul?**

• **How far do you think Jesus would go to have a relationship with you?**

Say: **Remember the verse for today from the 23rd Psalm: "Surely your goodness and unfailing love will pursue me all the days of my life."**

Ask: • **How did you see this verse at work in what happened to Saul?**

• **What's it like to know that Jesus loves you enough to pursue you?**

Say: **Jesus wanted to have a relationship with Saul, and he wants to have a relationship with you. And he went to some really big trouble to prove it.**

Jesus pursued Saul, and he pursues you. All you have to do to respond to Jesus is believe in him, just like Saul did.

No matter what you've done—and remember, Saul had done some pretty bad stuff—Jesus wants to be your friend. All you have to do is believe in him.

It may be tempting to jump in and offer groups advice. But resist the urge. Be ready to help if kids truly need it, but letting kids come up with ideas on their own helps cement the learning.

It's okay if two groups decide to present the same way. Their presentations will still be different and unique. Also, you can give groups more time to work on their presentations if you'd like.

Depending on your church's salvation doctrine, this might be a good time to talk to kids about a faith decision.

SCENIC ROUTE →

Let kids know that you'll be available after class to talk with any child who wants to know more about believing in Jesus.

FUN FACT

The expression "about face" comes from the military command for troops in formation to turn clockwise 180 degrees.

ADVENTURES IN GROWING

(10 minutes)

About Face!

This experience will help kids discover that they can change their ways, just as Saul did.

Say: **After Saul met Jesus, his life changed in a huge way. He went from being a guy who tried to put Christians in jail to a guy who tried to get everyone to believe in Jesus. His behavior changed. He basically did a complete "about face." That means he turned around and went in the opposite direction. Let's see what that's like.**

Have kids scatter around the room, facing in different directions. Then say: **I'm going to call out a few situations that kids your age might go through. When I start talking, you'll begin taking baby steps directly ahead of you. Just as in real life, you may bump into someone, or you may have to stop to let someone else by. That's okay.**

After each situation I'll say, "But if you knew Jesus in this situation, here's how your behavior might change." Then one of you has to call out what you might do differently in that situation once you knew Jesus. Afterward everyone take baby steps in a new direction.

When everyone understands the directions, say the following scenarios. Pause after each one until someone gives an appropriate answer. Then continue.

• **You were supposed to study for a history test, but you watched your favorite TV show instead. Now it's test time and you don't know the answers. You can see the answers of the person next to you. You start to copy the first answer. But if you knew Jesus in this situation, here's how your behavior might change.**

• **Your good friend made you mad last week, so you've been avoiding him. Now today at your lunch table, a few of the real popular kids are pointing at him and making fun of his clothes. You start to laugh, too. But if you knew Jesus in this situation, here's how your behavior might change.**

• **Your family's cat is always jumping on the dining room table and getting in trouble for it. You accidentally break your mom's vase on the table. You start to blame it on the cat. But if you knew Jesus in this situation, here's how your behavior might change.**

Thanks kids for their participation and answers. Say: **Like Saul, we can change our behavior once we get to know Jesus. ◐God is always with us. He's always rooting for us to make the right choices and do the** right things. Even when we sin and do bad things, like Saul did, Jesus doesn't stop loving us. He just keeps loving us and pursuing us.

Like today's verse says, "Surely your goodness and unfailing love will pursue me all the days of my life." Jesus pursued Saul, and he pursues us—all because he loves us. He wants to be with us every day, to help us do the right things and to show us how much he loves us.

I don't know about you, but I'm so glad that God is always with us!

**SOUVENIRS** (10 minutes)
Now and Then
This experience will help kids see that Jesus wants to be a part of their lives—for the rest of their lives.

Items to Pack: Bibles, copies of the "Now and Then" handout on page 105, pens, pencils, fine-tipped markers

Give each pair a Bible, and have kids read Psalm 23:6a with their partners.

Ask: • **How does this verse relate to what we read about Saul in the Bible today?**

• **Why is this verse important for your life?**

Give each child a copy of the "Now and Then" handout on page 105. Set out pens, pencils, and fine-tipped markers for kids to share.

Say: **On the handout, you'll see two picture frames. Follow the directions under each frame.**

When kids have finished writing and drawing, say: **Put your handouts in your Travel Journal to remind you that** **God is always with us. He loves you so much that he wants to be a part of your life—a big and important part—from now on. Let's thank Jesus for loving us that much.**

HOME AGAIN PRAYER (10 minutes)
Use this experience to reinforce the fact that Jesus is with us wherever we go and whatever we do.

Form a circle.

Say: **Today we learned that** **God is always with us. That means 24/7. And that means 24 hours a day, seven days a week. And that means all the time.**

Take a few moments to think of all the things you do and all the places you go in a typical week. Maybe you take the bus to school, you

sit in class, you go to soccer practice or piano lessons, you hang out at your friend's house, you go to the movies, you eat dinner with your family, you brush your teeth at night. And those are probably just a few of the things you do!

Let's hold hands and thank Jesus for being with us in all those places, as we do all of these things. We'll go around the circle, and we'll each thank Jesus for being with us either in a specific place or while doing a specific thing. We'll keep going around the circle two or three times. I'll start.

Pray: **Thank you, Jesus, for being with me when I teach at church.** Then go around the circle at least twice, having each person add a prayer. If kids want to "pass," they can squeeze the next person's hand. Close by thanking Jesus for loving us so much that he wants to always be with us.

Draw a picture of what you think you might be doing in 10 years.
Then write a thank you to God for being with you then.

Draw a picture of yourself doing something this week.
Then write a thank you to God for being with you this week.

13 The House of the Lord Forever

Pathway Point: God promises us eternal life.

The experiences in this book have been designed for multi-age groups. Select from the experiences, or adapt them as needed.

In-Focus Verse: "And I will live in the house of the Lord forever" (Psalm 23:6b).

Travel Itinerary

The kids in your group may have a hard time with a few of today's concepts. That's okay—so do adults! After all, the concept of eternity can be daunting to the human mind. Also, kids might think of the "house of the Lord" as an actual church building. (Thankfully, that's an easy misunderstanding to correct.) And "living water"? That's an abstract thought for kids who tend to be concrete thinkers.

Use today's adventure as a springboard for discussion—a place for kids to start thinking of a lifelong and eternal relationship with our loving God. Reinforce with your kids how loving God is, and how much he desires a relationship with each one of them. In fact, he desires it so much that he was willing to send his only Son to show us the way.

DEPARTURE PRAYER (up to 5 minutes)

Bring kids together.

Say: **During the last few months we've learned a lot from Psalm 23 about all the ways that God watches over us and loves us. Today we'll see that this psalm ends with the most beautiful of God's many promises to us.** God promises us eternal life.

Say: **The word *eternal* means never-ending. Let's discuss that a little more.**

Ask: • **What can you think of that goes on and on without stopping?**

• **What's something you love to do that you wish you could do forever?**

• **What's something boring you have to do that *seems* like it goes on forever?**

Have kids form a circle. Say: **Look at how we're standing. Now I**

106

realize that we don't form a perfect circle, but we're still a pretty good circle, right? Here's something that goes on without stopping: A circle has no beginning and no end. That's kind of like what being "eternal" means—no beginning and no end. God is eternal—he's always existed and he always will exist. I know that's hard to imagine, but God said it so we know it's true. We may not fully understand it until we get to heaven, but that's okay.

In fact, heaven is what I want to talk about today. That's where we'll spend eternal life—if we believe in Jesus. Let's find out more. But first, let's thank God for his promise of eternal life.

Explain that you'll start the prayer by thanking God for Jesus, our way to heaven. Then you'll take the hand of the person to your right. He or she will thank God for Jesus and take the next person's hand. If kids don't want to pray out loud, they can "pass" by squeezing the next person's hand. Continue around the circle until everyone's holding hands. Then close the prayer by asking God to help each person in the circle grow closer to Jesus.

 (15 minutes)
Never-Ending Love
Kids will make reminders of how God's love for them never ends.

Items to Pack: Paper, scissors, tape, pens or pencils

Ahead of time, cut sheets of paper into strips about 2 x 11 inches. You'll need at least two strips for each person, including yourself.

Gather kids together. Set out the paper strips, pens or pencils, and tape.

Say: ◖**God promises us eternal life. We already know that eternal means never-ending. Let's make something that will help us understand the idea of never-ending.** Give each child one of the paper strips you prepared earlier.

Say: **Look at your paper strip—turn it over—really inspect it and decide how many sides it has. If everyone agrees that our paper strips have two sides, let's try a little experiment. I'll demonstrate, and you do the same thing I do. Find a partner and help each other. Take turns making what I make. I'll show you how.** Hold your paper strip up by the ends, for everyone to see.

Say: **I'm going to twist my paper strip one time, and then I'll tape the ends together. Will someone hand me the tape, please?**

Twist your paper strip 180 degrees to form a Mobius strip. Have a volunteer help you securely tape the ends together. Then go around the room, helping kids as needed to make their own Mobius strips.

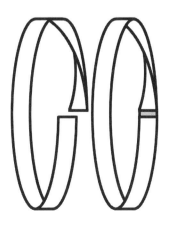

If you have mostly younger children in your group, you can skip the section where kids make a double strip.

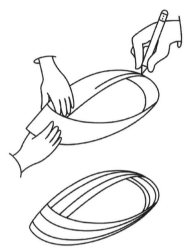

You'll probably want to help kids start the cuts on the two lines. If there are any mishaps, help kids make new Mobius strips, or have extras handy that you made beforehand.

Items to Pack: Bibles, small salted pretzels, napkins, cups of water

Say: **Great job! What you made is called a Mobius strip. It's named after the guy who discovered how to make one. Now remember, your original paper strip had two sides, right? But a Mobius strip actually only has one side. I'll prove it to you.**

Give each person a pen or pencil. Demonstrate how to place the point of the pen or pencil in the middle of the strip, and then draw a steady line, without stopping, until you reach the starting point again. Help kids as needed.

Say: **See? You only drew one line, and it goes all the way around your Mobius strip. It only has one never-ending side. Pretty cool!**

Ask: • **What surprised you about this activity?**

• **What do you find surprising about the idea of eternal life?**

Say: **Now let's try something even more amazing. We'll each need to make another Mobius strip.** Pause as kids each make another Mobius strip, helping kids as necessary. When everyone has another strip made, continue.

Say: **This time, draw two lines around your Mobius strip, like this.** Demonstrate how to draw the two lines. Use the margin drawing as a guide.

Say: **Now let's find out what happens when you cut the Mobius strip apart on these two lines.**

When everyone has drawn the two lines, demonstrate how to poke a small hole on one of the lines, and carefully cut all the way around on that line—don't quite complete the cut, though. Let the result surprise kids. The Mobius strip will actually form two linked strips.

When kids have finished and are holding their linked strips, continue.

Ask: • **What do you think about what happened to your Mobius strip?**

• **How do you think that might be like or unlike your reaction to what eternal life is like?**

Say: **If we believe in Jesus, we can have eternal life with him in heaven some day. We can't know exactly what that will be like, but the Bible does give us a few clues. We'll look at some of them in just a few minutes.**

But right now, let's hear—right from Jesus—how to get to heaven.

STORY EXCURSION (20 minutes)
Living Water
This experience will teach kids that Jesus offers us the kind of love that satisfies our every need.

Open your Bible to John 4:1-42, and show kids the passage.

Say: **Before we get started in the Bible today, let's have a little snack.**

Give each person a napkin and a few small salted pretzels to eat.

Say: **Before we read the Bible, let's try something.** Have kids form pairs, and have partners stand facing each other. The person in each pair wearing the most green will go first. That person will put both hands behind his or her back, and hold up a number of fingers. The other partner will try to guess how many unseen fingers are being held up.

Then partners will switch roles. Have each pair play several rounds. After a few minutes, call time.

Ask: • **Why couldn't everyone guess correctly each time?**

Say: **Today's Bible passage tells us that Jesus knew all about someone—and he wasn't guessing. Knowing everything about us is just one more thing Jesus can do. That's pretty amazing, I'll admit.**

Form four groups, and make sure each group has at least one Bible. Assign each group one of the following passages:

- John 4:1-12
- John 4:13-18
- John 4:19-26
- John 4:27-30; 39-42

Explain that each group will read its part of the Bible and then decide how they can silently act out what happened. Everyone else will try to guess what happened. Say that after others have guessed, the group can tell what actually happened in that part of the Bible.

Say: **This is a tough assignment, so I guess you'll need some nourishment. Here are a few more pretzels.** Give each person a few more pretzels to eat.

Give groups about five to seven minutes to prepare their presentations. Then let groups silently act out their sections of the Bible as others guess what actually happened. Let groups confirm or explain the action in their parts of the Bible.

After each presentation, give kids each another pretzel to eat.

After all groups have finished presenting, lead kids in a round of applause for everyone's participation.

Make a show of swallowing. Say: **Thanks for presenting the Bible in such interesting ways.** Swallow dramatically again. **Excuse me—my mouth seems kind of dry. I don't know about you, but those salty pretzels made me thirsty. I'd love to drink a cup of cool, refreshing water.**

Ask: • **Why does water taste so good when you're really thirsty?**

Some children have food allergies that can be dangerous. Know your children, and consult with parents about allergies their children may have. Also, read food labels carefully, as hidden ingredients can cause allergy-related problems.

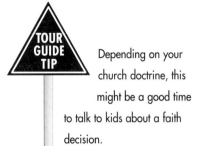
Depending on your church doctrine, this might be a good time to talk to kids about a faith decision.

• **What's the thirstiest you could ever imagine being?**

Say: **For me, I think being stranded on a desert in the hot noonday sun would make me the thirstiest. All I'd want is a drink of water!**

Ask: • **What do you think "living water" means?**

• **Why do you think Jesus compared himself to living water?**

Say: **Imagine that your soul—the part of you that makes you who you are—is thirsty.**

Ask: • **What kinds of things are most people thirsty for in their souls?**

• **What are some ways people try to find these things for themselves?**

Say: **This is where Jesus comes in. Jesus loves us so much that he gave his life on the cross to take the punishment for our sins. He did that because he loves us. He accepts us—just as we are. He brings us peace because he's there to help us no matter what happens. Only Jesus can give us eternal life, and only Jesus can make our souls stop being thirsty.**

Ask: • **What's something you can do this week to help you remember the living water you have from Jesus?**

• **How can you tell someone else this week about the living water Jesus offers?**

Ask a few children to help you distribute small cups of water to everyone.

Say: **Just as physical water makes the thirst in our throats go away, Jesus' living water makes the thirst in our souls go away. The way to get the living water Jesus offers is simply by believing in him and accepting how much he loves you.**

Say: **Every time you're thirsty this week, stop and think about the living water you can have from Jesus. And if you happen to see someone else drinking water, tell them what you learned from the Bible.**

(10 minutes)
Picture Perfect
Kids will discover more about the eternal life God promises to us.

Ahead of time, write each of these Scripture references on a separate slip of paper: John 3:16; John 11:25; Romans 6:23; and Romans 10:9. Put the paper slips in a bowl or bag.

Set out poster board, paper, scissors, a variety of colored markers, colored

Items to Pack: Bibles, poster board, paper, bowl or bag, scissors, a variety of colored markers, colored pencils, other simple art supplies

pencils, and whatever other simple art supplies you have handy. Kids can stay in the same four groups from the previous activity. Make sure each group has at least one Bible.

Say: **The most amazing thing of all about Jesus is the way he makes it possible for us to live with him in heaven. I'll show you what I mean. The person in your group wearing the most red can come up and choose a slip of paper. But don't open it until I say so.** Have group representatives choose paper slips. When kids are back in their groups, continue.

Say: **On your paper slip is a verse from the Bible. In your group, look up the verse and talk about what that verse means to you. Once you've decided what it means, work together to create a poster that will help everyone else understand it.**

For example, if the verse talks about Jesus forgiving our sins, maybe you could draw a child holding a broken vase, and the boy and his mom are praying.

Have groups read their paper slips and find their Scripture verses. All the verses have to do with today's topic of eternal life. Circulate around the room to offer help as needed. If kids seem stumped, you might offer the following ideas to get them started.

• John 3:16. Kids could draw hands holding the earth, and draw a heart over each country to show that God loves all people and sent Jesus to save them.

• John 11:25. Kids could draw the empty tomb, or they could draw what they think heaven will look like.

• Romans 6:23. Kids could draw a big wrapped gift on one side of the paper, and a circle containing the word *death* crossed out (as in a "no smoking" sign).

• Romans 10:9. Kids could draw someone holding a big megaphone, with the words of the verse coming out of the megaphone.

When kids have finished drawing, have each group explain its picture. Then have someone from the group read the verse aloud. After all the groups have presented their pictures, lead everyone in a round of applause for all the great artwork.

Say: **Thanks for helping us understand more about how** **God promises us eternal life through Jesus. Take just another minute or so to discuss in your group how you can use your group's verse in your life this week.** After a minute or two, ask volunteers to share their answers with the large group.

Then say: **Let's use this next experience to make sure what we just learned sticks in our brains.**

Items to Pack: Bibles, copies of the "Living Water" handout on page 114, pens or markers, scissors, paper, glue sticks

(10 minutes)

Living Water

Kids will see that Jesus promises us the living water of eternal life.

Set out paper, scissors, pens or markers, and glue sticks. Give each person a copy of the "Living Water" handout on page 114.

Say: **Today we're learning that** ⬤**God promises us eternal life. And we can only get that eternal life through believing in Jesus.**

In the Bible, the woman at the well ran and told lots of people about Jesus, and many of those people believed in Jesus that day. Now think about what qualities you need so you can tell other people about Jesus and the eternal life he offers. When you've come up with what would help you to do this, write these things on the front of the well on your handout. No one else will see this because you're going to cover it up.

When kids have finished, have each one cut a piece of paper to fit over the picture of the well and glue it to the well on the bottom and the two sides, leaving the top open as a "pocket." Then have kids each cut a few paper slips and write on each one the name of someone they can tell about Jesus this week. Kids will put the paper slips into the well.

When everyone has finished, say: **Take your wells home with you in your Travel Journals today as reminders to ask God for what you need, so you can follow through on telling people about Jesus. If you need a little nudge, just pull out one of the paper slips!**

Before we close, let's take a minute to thank God for promising us eternal life—the chance to live in the house of the Lord forever.

HOME AGAIN PRAYER

(10 minutes)

Use this experience to reinforce with kids how deeply God loves them and how much he desires an eternal relationship with them.

Give each person a white foam cup and a permanent marker. Have kids write the words of today's Key Verse around the middle of the cup: "And I will live in the house of the Lord forever."

Then have kids stand in a circle with their cups. Say: **Because we learned about living water, I'm going to pour a sip of cool water in your cup for you to enjoy.** Go around the circle and pour a sip of water into each child's cup as you say: "[name of child], **God promises you eternal life.**"

Items to Pack: Bibles, white foam cups, permanent markers, pitcher of water

When you've gone around the circle, close with this prayer. Pray: **God, thank you for sending Jesus, our good shepherd, to bring us living water. If we believe in him, we can have eternal life with you in heaven. Help us tell others about Jesus this week. And help us remember all the ways you watch over us and love us. In Jesus' name. Amen.**

Encourage kids to take their cups home. Say that every time they use them, they can remember the living water Jesus offers to us.

For more amazing resources

visit us at
group.com...

...or call us at
1-800-447-1070!

Incredible things will happen